TABOOED JUNG

MARGINALITY AS POWER

Also by the same author

BLAKE AND THE ASSIMILATION OF CHAOS
COLERIDGE'S THEORY OF IMAGINATION TODAY (*editor*)
SHELLEY'S AMBIVALENCE

TABOOED JUNG
Marginality as Power

Christine Gallant
Professor of English
Georgia State University

NEW YORK UNIVERSITY PRESS
Washington Square, New York

First published in the U.S.A. in 1996 by
NEW YORK UNIVERSITY PRESS
Washington Square
New York, N.Y. 10003

Library of Congress Cataloging-in-Publication Data
Gallant. Christine, 1940–
Tabooed Jung : marginality as power / Christine Gallant
p. cm.
Includes bibliographical references and index.
SIBN 0–8147–3087–6
1. Jungian psychology. 2. Psychoanalysis—History. 3. Jung, C. G. (Carl Gustav), 1875–1961. 4 Freud, Sigmund, 1856–1939.
I. Title.
BF173.G34 1996
150.19'54—dc20 95–51264
CIP

Printed in Great Britain

Contents

Part I
Marginalization

Introduction

> Disciplines constitute a system of control in the production of discourse . . . determining the conditions under which it may be employed, imposing a certain number of rules upon those individuals who employ it, thus denying access to everyone else. . . .
>
> Not all areas of discourse are equally open and penetrable; some are forbidden territory (differentiated and differentiating), while others are virtually open to the winds and stand, without any prior restriction, open to all.
>
> Michel Foucault
> *The Archaeology of Knowledge*

Avoided with a formulaic dread of his 'mysticism,' unread lest the contagion of his thoughts be transmitted and his influence infect the orthodox, anathemized as all that is a danger to the social cohesiveness of the group, Jung has always been a tabooed object for the psychoanalytic Movement.

The history of his relationship with Freud and the theory of psychology he developed provoke a different reaction to Jung than to the other dissidents. Adler, Rank, Ferenczi, Reich, and Horney also left Freud's orbit. But only the response to Jung is emotionally toned in the way described by Freud himself when he writes about taboo in *Totem and Taboo:* 'It has about it a sense of something unapproachable . . . principally expressed in prohibitions and restrictions. Our collocation 'holy dread' would often coincide in meaning with 'taboo'.[1]

But the 'holy dread' comes from a more fundamental transgression than that of theory, although it is Jung's theory of archetypes and the collective unconscious that has seemed to Freudians most to define everything that Freudian psychoanalytic theory is not. Rather it is due to the fact that Jung, more than any of the other dissidents, came close to and then wounded the person identified with the Movement. He challenged the *mana* of Freud.

One sees here the emotional ambivalence that Freud thought fueled the taboo: the unacknowledged desire to perform the tabooed act checked by the detestation of it, so that the real reason for the taboo is 'the risk of imitation, which would quickly lead to the dissolution of the community.'[2]

This can be seen clearly enough in the events of the formative years of the Movement. Key factors in the situation then were the envy of Jung's closeness to Freud by other disciples who were also competing for Freud's attention, and the furtively expressed desire for their own independence from Freud – and also the genuine wish to protect Freud from a repetition of the earlier 'creative illness' he experienced when he broke with Fliess. Certainly Jung functioned as a tabooed object for the 'Committee' of five psychoanalytic pioneers that quickly formed around Freud after his rupture with Jung. This Committee acted as Freud says a primitive society does to guard its ruler and his *mana*. This is fairly predictable.

But it is arresting that this emotional response has remained more or less characteristic of the Movement ever since. Jung's experience with Freud should be instructive for those who are now looking at the Movement from an external viewpoint, for the pattern of events leading up to the split portended the orthodoxy deliberately imposed afterwards. Indeed, these events *precipitated* the orthodoxy.

But beyond that, Jung's situation predicted the recent increasing disenchantment with Freud and things Freudian. The dynamics of Jung's exclusion from the group have been re-enacted by later players. The fundamental criticisms that Jung made of Freudian theory are delivered again today. The theories and findings of the mature Jung and later Jungians are congenial with contemporary psychoanalytic work. Yet little of this goes recognized by today's critics – many of whom would probably bristle at the suggestion that there is less difference between Jung and themselves than they think.

Jung's entire case is a paradigm of the 'production of discourse'.

1

The Banned Voice

The history of the friendship between Jung and Freud from 1906 to 1913 has been generally known, but the publication of *The Freud/Jung Letters* in 1974 revealed more of the inside story.[1]

Jung first wrote to Freud to praise his innovative psychoanalytic ideas and to present his own paper on something new: word association experiments. Freud at that point was fifty and securely established, if controversial. He had laid the foundations of psychoanalysis, and gathered the loyal together into a group. Jung himself was thirty-one, chief assistant to the prominent Bleuler in Zurich, and had already gained his reputation by developing the technique of the word association test that he used to detect the presence of what he later termed 'complexes'. If the two men were not exactly on equal footing, still Jung had his own assured standing.

Their personal rapport grew rapidly, and Jung's position with Freud grew closer. There were many references in letters on both sides during these years of 1906–9 to Jung as 'son' and to Jung's 'father-complex'. (Humorous references? Pleased? Self-ironic? Defensive? Freud's 'fathering-complex'?) During this time Jung was busy starting his psychoanalytic practice in Zurich as well as beginning his researches into mythology.

Jung's letters then showed the tentative explorations of possibilities that later would lead to his mature system of thought, reading as if he was throwing out line after line into a great unknown ocean. He did not quite see the theoretical connections yet between the different materials that caught his attention from his patients' experiences and dreams, from world religions, from classical mythology, and from art and literature. They all interested him equally. Nothing was dismissed as *inherently* irrelevant or unworthy of serious consideration.

However, Freud revealed in his letters the increasingly uneasy feeling that Jung was straying into territories that should be forbidden to the psychoanalyst. As Jung unfolded his developing theories in front of Freud, Freud used the same kind of words again and again to dismiss them: 'spook complex', 'fairytale', 'mysticism', 'occultism.' He used these terms at the times when Jung in some way was suggesting his growing autonomy. They came to seem like an attempt to control.

In Freud's letters to Jung between 1909 and 1912 one can see the definition forming of what is to be considered taboo for psychoanalysis – and it was everything that Jung was finding most exciting and full of possibilities. Freud's designations of Jungian theory have been repeated consistently down to the present to sum up Jung and all that is mistaken about his analytical psychology: Freud created the language to describe what was taboo.

In April 1909 Jung wrote to Freud after an incident in Vienna in which they had been discussing precognition and parapsychology. Freud had dismissed the whole subject as 'nonsensical', just as the bookcase gave a loud report. Jung predicted a second such noise, which immediately followed. Freud 'stared aghast' at him.[2] In Jung's letter, he self-ironically referred to his 'spookery' in the incident.[3] Freud answered by taking up Jung's term with crushing literalness: 'I shall receive further news of your investigation of the spook complex with the interest one accords a charming delusion in which one does not oneself participate.'[4]

The real subject of both letters, though, was Jung's supposed 'father complex' in relation to Freud, as Jung predicted the son's adult independence and Freud predicted parricide. A certain fulfillment of the Oedipal talion law – for both son and father – seemed to be taking place in these letters.

For his part, Jung passed from alluding to his own 'spookery' to adding: 'That last evening with you [when he had so disconcerted Freud in Vienna] has, most happily, freed me inwardly from the oppressive sense of your paternal authority. My unconscious celebrated this impression with a great dream.'[5] Freud did not receive this 'impression' with as much élan. He answered: 'It is strange that on the very evening when I formally adopted you as eldest son and anointed you – *in partibus infidelium* [in the land of unbelievers] – as my successor and crown prince, you should have divested me of my paternal dignity, which divesting seems to have given you as much pleasure as I, on the contrary, derived from the investiture of your person.'[6]

Freud's term here, 'crown prince,' has long been used more or less sardonically by Freudian partisans to refer to Jung and his disloyal attempt at regicide, rather as if Freud were laying bare Jung's covert grandiose ambitions. But what is odd here is that Freud should find Jung's reaction strange, and call him to task for finding any 'pleasure' in resisting 'the investiture of [his] person' when *Freud* had decided on the coronation. It is also noteworthy that in a letter deriding Jung's 'spook-complex,' Freud used religious language to describe his own actions (as he often did in other letters to Jung): 'anoint', '*in partibus infidelium*'. It is the highest ecclesiastical authority who coronates the new king.

Jung took a month to reply (an action that always nettled Freud), then opened with the remark: 'I have not gone over to any system yet and shall also guard against putting my trust in those spooks.'[7]

By 1909 Jung's letters to Freud began to suggest his desire for more autonomy in the rather indirect way of slipping revealing sentences midway through long paragraphs or near the end of long letters, or by couching them in a jocular tone. This is seen most obviously in Jung's running comments about his theoretical ideas just developing, that were clearly growing further and further away from Freud's governing ideas that the libido is exclusively sexual in nature and the neuroses rooted solely in the individual's immediate experiences. It is also to be seen in his quick, rather testy rejoinders to Freud's sarcasms and an occasional over-sensitivity to Freud's criticisms.

Freud responded by tightening the reins: by alluding in an ironic way to the past 'traitor' Fliess, by ridiculing Jung's diverging concepts, or by emphasizing the need for solidarity among the practitioners of the new 'science' of psychoanalysis. The letters of both men from this point until their break in 1913 include revealing parapraxes.

Thus in January Jung wrote, 'Your meddling in my editorial activities [as editor of the *Jahrbuch*] is of course quite acceptable to me as I still feel too firm in the saddle,' when he intended to write '. . . as I still *don't* feel too firm in the saddle'.[8]

In March, Freud dropped an unmistakably warning mention of Wilhelm Fliess. Fliess and Freud became close friends in 1887, when Freud had just established his own practice and was a lecturer at the University of Vienna. Their letters, published in full for the first time in 1985, suggest that at the emotional level at least there probably was a homoerotic tinge to their relationship.[9] Fliess's withdrawal from their friendship and then final break caused Freud to enter what he later called his 'creative illness'; and Fliess's name became synonymous with Judas for Freud's later circle.

Freud's earlier mentions of Fliess to Jung were quite factual.[10] But in 1909, the allusion was accusatory and taken as such by Jung. Freud evidently had telegrammed Jung to inquire about his tardiness in correspondence. When Jung at once wrote a conciliatory letter, Freud replied: 'I evidently still have traumatic hyperaesthesia toward dwindling correspondence. I remember its genesis well (Fliess) and should not like to repeat such an experience unawares.'[11]

Jung wrote in return: 'You may rest assured, not only now but for the future, that nothing Fliess-like is going to happen.'[12] Jung mentioned Fliess again in April, when he wrote to Freud about the 'spook' incident in Vienna: 'It seemed to me that my spookery struck you as altogether too stupid and perhaps unpleasant because of the Fliess analogy.'[13] This allusion may have been a contributory cause of Freud's answering 'crown prince' letter.

Again and again, Jung threw out hints in these letters from 1909 of his evolving analytic theory; and again and again, he implied that his own concept of libido was perhaps not Freud's. In June, he concluded a letter: 'Only when these general foundations have been laid can I launch into the bigger problems of the metamorphosis of libido in Dem. pr, [dementia praecox, the earlier name for schizophrenia].'[14] In October he wrote, predicting what turned out to be true of his future work: 'I am obsessed by the thought of one day writing a comprehensive account of this whole field, after years of fact-finding and preparation, of course. The net should be cast wide. Archaeology or rather mythology has got me in its grip, it's a mine of marvelous material.'[15] The letters during this time relating to Jung's developing analytic theories shuttled back and forth.

Meanwhile, Viennese politicking went on in an increasingly internecine way as the loyal maneuvered for priority with Freud, and generally tightened their ranks. As Freud's friendship with Jung grew, so did the irritation of his Viennese followers who felt rather pre-empted by the 'Zurich school'. When Freud proposed in 1910 that an international psychoanalytic association be formed with Jung as permanent president, his Viennese adherents protested bitterly. Finally a compromise was worked out and Jung was made president for two years only, although Freud's decision still rankled with the Viennese group.

In mid-1911 one of Freud's favorites, Alfred Adler, parted with Freud over theory: specifically, over Freud's concept of the libido. Adler's papers presented to Freud's discussion group in Vienna (the Vienna Society) made it clear that he was more concerned with the ego and its conscious processes than he was with the unconscious and the libido.[16] Adler resigned as chairman of the Vienna Society, and Wilhelm Stekel resigned in support. About this time, Jung was re-elected President of the International Psychoanalytic Society. So Freud was particularly alert to any signs that Jung might be straying from the preserve as well.

Jung's letters of 1911, otherwise full of the business of coordinating the Movement and dealing with various supporters and critics, increasingly included asides about his fascination with mythology, 'wandering alone through a strange country'.[17] This last confidence, written with the flush of intellectual discovery ('and seeing wonderful things that no-one has seen before'), provoked Freud to refer dismissively to this 'fairytale forest feeling'.[18]

In the way that is characteristic of his later syncretic method, Jung's discoveries in classical and Eastern mythologies led him to explore the related field of astrology, a far less 'respectable' scholarly field than comparative mythology. In mid-1911 he wrote to Freud: 'Occultism is another field we shall have to conquer – with the aid of the libido theory, it seems to me. [Another sign he was straying.] At the moment I am looking into astrology, which seems indispensable for a proper understanding of mythology.'[19] Jung would seem to be using the word 'occultism' in its literal sense of secret knowledge communicated only to the initiated, that derives from the ancient sciences. Astrology thus was the parent of astronomy.

But Freud seized upon this word as an unintentionally negative self-revelation. Upon receiving this letter, Freud wrote to Ferenczi: 'Jung writes to me that we must conquer the field of occultism . . . it is a dangerous expedition.'[20] To Jung, he wrote: 'I am aware that you are driven by innermost inclination to the study of the occult and I am sure you will return home richly laden. . . . You will be accused of mysticism, but the reputation you won with the *Dementia* will hold up for quite some time against that.'[21] Decidedly a double-edged remark, considering that Jung's professional reputation had been secured by his publications on dementia praecox.

A month later, Jung wrote of a patient whose case seemed to confirm astrological theory.[22] Freud returned to the charge of 'occultism,' and then followed in the next paragraph by dismissing Jung's analysis of fantasies in dementia praecox as really being nothing more than daydreams.[23] Evidently the reputation that Jung 'won' is already showing signs of not 'hold[ing] up'.

Yet things were not as clear-cut as they might seem: Jung, the occultist, and Freud, the rationalist. Freud had had his own occult beliefs for some time before this, and would for some time after. Fliess's rather peculiar theories about periodicity seem to have struck an answering chord in Freud's own number superstition, in part explaining why Freud during their friendship was so slow to question Fliess's obsessive theories about numbers influencing human biology.[24]

For many years, Freud felt that he would die at the age of fifty-one and then later sixty-two, and combinations of these ciphers seemed ominously significant to him. During the years he was writing to Jung and for many afterwards, Freud considered the possibility of the existence of what he called 'thought-transference,' or telepathy.[25] In December 1910, he wrote to Ferenczi that he had met with Jung and discussed Freud's 'worry about what to do with the matter of telepathy'. Freud was still interested enough in the subject by 1921 to write a paper for a small group of sympathizers on 'Psychoanalysis and Telepathy,' although it was only published posthumously.

His famous essay 'The Uncanny' showed the deep pull that the 'mystical' and 'occult' had for him.[26] He carefully began : 'The writer of the present contribution must himself plead guilty to a special obtuseness in the matter. . . . It is long since he has experienced or heard of anything which has given him an uncanny impression';[27] but soon he was relating various 'uncanny' experiences involving number superstition and dèja vu that he himself had. Originally written in 1913 and then rewritten in 1919, the essay's very existence shows a fascination with the occult that Freud attempted to dissipate through analysis of its origins (which for him of course must be the original 'uncanny' maternal genitals).

During late 1911 and early 1912 Jung was preoccupied with writing *Wandlungen und Symbole der Libido,* which later became his first major work, *Symbols of Transformation.* This long, massively documented, swirlingly-styled book was his first attempt to organize the welter of mythological materials he had discovered, so that they accorded with a rudimentary theory of archetypes. Freud himself was writing *Totem and Taboo.*

Jung had been including news of the various mythological treasures he was excavating in his letters to Freud through this period, though this lessened during the book's composition. It is apparent from Freud's letters that the more he heard the less he liked, for Jung's book centered on a diametrically different way of conceptualizing the libido from Freudian theory. During this period Jung was also maintaining his regular psychoanalytic practice, as well as keeping up his duties as President of the International Psychoanalytic Society. For these and probably other more private reasons, his letters to Freud usually were written at least ten days to two weeks after receiving those of Freud rather than being the return torpedoes that Freud sent to him.

Their letters of January and February of 1912 showed the early signs of what was coming in September of that year, when Jung published his book and thus made public and permanent his break with Freudian theory. Freud's first letter of the year, and the last one of 1911, chided Jung for not writing for several weeks. This silence should not have surprised Freud too much. The last letter he had written to Jung said of the libido-theory just advanced by Jung in his previous letter:

> I am all in favor of your attacking the libido question and I myself am expecting much light from your efforts. Often, it seems, I can go for a long while without feeling the need to clarify an obscure point, and then one day I am compelled to by the pressure of facts or by the influence of someone else's ideas.[28]

A catty putdown.

This was written on December 17. On December 28, Freud sent a short letter of regards at the close of the year.[29] On December 31, he wrote: 'I am writing to you once again this year, because I can't always wait for you to answer and prefer to write when I have time and am in the mood.'[30] He concluded with a sentence showing that he saw there might be a reason for the silence, for it began: 'If you really feel any resentment towards me. . .'[31] Jung replied on January 2 with a letter sending 'heartiest New Year wishes,'[32] then a week later (still not exactly speedily) another that noted: 'I do not claim any general validity for my views, so there is no reason for "resentment".'[33] Freud replied by return mail (for letters were delivered in Zurich one day after they were posted in Vienna) and ended: 'With kind regards, good wishes and a request for news at an early date.'[34]

Jung replied two weeks later, apologetically, and signed off self-ironically: 'This letter is quite vacuous. At the moment I am not giving out any libido, it's all going into my work [his book-manuscript].'[35] By return mail Freud sent a brief note: 'I have no wish to intrude on your concentration but merely wish to inform you. . .'[36] Three weeks later Jung wrote, again pleading the reasonable excuse of writing a long complicated book.[37]

Freud wrote, again by return mail, with resentful omens of what was in store for Jung: 'I was very glad to receive a letter from you. I am not fond of breaking habits and find no triumph in it. [Here he slipped into a parapraxis, and actually wrote, '. . . and find no triumph in you.'] Wrenched out of the habit, I no longer remember what I have told you, and besides, I still want to be considerate of your work.' But two sentences later, he wrote: '. . . you hide behind your religious-libidinal cloud.'[38]

This stung Jung, as one can see in his letter a week later where he repeats the phrase, 'religious-libidinal cloud,' and then excuses himself by declaring that he simply has been unable to explain his ideas fully in letters. However, he added, 'it is an elaboration of all the problems that arise out of the mother-incest libido, or rather, the libido-cathected mother-imago.'[39]

Things were coming out in the open, and Freud replied to the muffled bugle-call at once by writing to turn the blame for Jung's 'reluctance' upon Jung, and then to imply that his own support was being withdrawn as a result: 'I took myself in hand and quickly turned off any excess libido. I was sorry to do so, yet glad to see how quickly I managed it.' And he concluded by reminding Jung of what should be his time-consuming responsibilities to the International Psychoanalytic Society: 'But it would be a severe blow to all of us if you were to draw the libido you require for your work from the Association. . .'[40] Jung, then, is not to develop theory or write books, as that is already being done for him?

Jung's answering letter (within only three days, for once), began: 'Your letter has made me very pensive.' Then he went on to answer Freud's charges, spelling out that he was in the middle of writing a book more than 300 pages long, adding that 'of course I have opinions which are not yours about the ultimate truths of psychoanalysis', and concluding with a quote from Nietzsche about the necessity for the pupil to become independent of his teacher.[41] All in all, it seems like an attempt to mollify in advance, for Jung knew what was coming.

Freud's counterattack was swift, and contained unmistakable warnings that Jung was in danger of being cast out. He conjured the dread name of Adler, and then sweetly inquired why Jung was so 'pensive'? 'Do you think I am looking for someone else capable of being my friend, my helper and my heir, or that I expect to find another so soon?' That present tense gave the warning.

So did a revealing parapraxis. Freud meant to write: 'You speak of the need for intellectual independence. . . But if a third party were to read this passage, he would ask me when I had tried to tyrannize you intellectually, and I should have to say: I don't know.' But what he actually wrote was: 'If a person were to read the passage, he would ask me *why* I had tried to tyrannize you intellectually. . .'[42]

Adler's name performed its magical function, and Jung declared: 'I haven't the slightest intention of imitating Adler.'[43] Peace prevailed for the rest of March and most of April. At the end of April, Freud mentioned that he was eager to read Jung's 'libido paper with its new concept of libido' since possibly Jung's 'Declaration of Independence' only referred to this specific theoretical point and not anything else. (However, calling a 300-page manuscript a 'paper' seems rather to underrate it.) He emphasized his broad-mindedness: 'You will see that I am quite capable of listening and accepting, or of waiting until an idea becomes clearer to me. . . . One learns little by little to renounce one's personality.'[44]

Jung took him up on it. He wrote one letter summarizing his basic position on the meaning of incest, and then another soon after elaborating on his points made there. He did so succinctly, even laconically, as if he were simply stating the worst to get it over with:

> Like you, I am absorbed in the incest problem and have come to conclusions which show incest primarily as a fantasy problem . . . . The tremendous role of the mother in mythology has a significance far outweighing the biological incest problem – a significance that amounts to pure fantasy. Kind regards, Most sincerely yours, Jung.[45]

This next to the last sentence shows how far he has gone from Freudian theory, for what he really meant was that the figure of the mother has an archetypal, not only a personal, significance. For once, there was no letter by return mail from Freud.

Jung returned to his subject with a letter devoted to his theory, rather than his usual kind of letter that set it forth apologetically or tacked it on to the end after the 'real' subject of Movement politics or business matters. He concluded: 'Evidently the object of the [incest] prohibition is not to prevent incest but to consolidate the family (or piety, or the social structure).'[46] Freud's entire Oedipal theory is thus disowned.

Freud's answering letter briefly set forth his 'observations' on what Jung wrote ('they are not refutations but should be taken merely as expressions of doubt'), and then passed on to business matters. Jung answered two days later, making his full 'Declaration of Independence'(*Freud's* term) as he gave the conclusions he had reached from his mythological studies: taboos do not have a biological origin for they are symbolic in nature. 'In my opinion the incest barrier can no more be explained by reduction to the possibility of real incest than the animal cult can be explained by reduction to real bestiality.' And he concluded with the modest wish: 'I hope I have expressed myself a bit more clearly this time.'[47]

He had. Freud responded with a parapraxis. He meant to write: 'What I still fail to understand is why you have abandoned the older view of the libido and what other origin and motivation the prohibition of incest can have.' What he actually wrote was '. . . why you have abandoned the older view and what other origin and motivation the prohibition of incest,' which shifts the emphasis onto Jung's abandonment and away from the theoretical question. Cutting sentences immediately followed: 'I value your letter for the warning it contains, and the reminder of my first big error, when I mistook fantasies for realities. I shall be careful and keep my eyes open every step of the way.' His use of the word 'fantasies' seems almost wilfully different from Jung's, who had intended the psychological rather than popular meaning of the word. He added that Jung's ideas have 'a disastrous similarity to a theorem of Adler's'.[48]

Jung's trepidation can be seen in his note that crossed this letter in the mail: 'I hope nothing untoward has happened that would account for your delay in answering my last letter. If I have the assurance that there are no weightier reasons behind the delay, I shall naturally go on waiting and not make any exorbitant demands on your time and nervous energy.'[49]

There followed the curious 'Kreuzlingen gesture,' as Jung called it. Freud visited the famed psychologist Binswanger for a few days in May at Kreuzlingen, forty miles from Zurich, and failed to call on Jung. Jung took it as a deliberate slight. Freud pointed out that if he were to visit Zurich he would have had to forgo one of his two days available to visit Binswanger (then suffering from cancer, unknown to Jung); and he did not ask Jung to come to Kreuzlingen 'because it is an imposition to ask anyone to spend a holiday in such a way if he has something better to do or wants to rest'.[50] But he had notified Jung of his visit in advance, and would have been glad if Jung had volunteered to come.

Jung evidently took this as a rationalization, for after five weeks he replied in July with a brief note: 'Until now I didn't know what to say your last letter. Now I can only say: I understand the Kreuzlingen gesture.'[51] In November when the International Psychoanalytic Association met for their Munich Conference, Freud and Jung talked over the 'Kreuzlingen gesture'. Jung agreed that he had been mistaken and apologized, and there was a brief – very brief – peace between them. But until then, the sense of injustice rankled on both sides.

During the period between July and November came the first overt sign that Jung was being made taboo by the community: the formation of the 'Secret Committee'. Ernest Jones first thought of such a committee in June when he was visiting Ferenczi in Venice, and he spoke about it to Freud when he saw him in Karlsbad in August.[52] This group was to be comprised of the most faithful of the faithful – Ernest Jones, Sandor Ferenczi, Otto Rank, Karl Abraham, and Hans Sachs – who would close ranks around Freud, guard the future theoretical development of psychoanalysis, and ward off any possible future defections.

Freud took to the idea at once, and felt that the existence of the committee would 'make living and dying easier for me'. Its first requirement, he agreed, was that 'this committee has to be *strictly secret* [italics his]'.[53] The following May Freud gave each member an intaglio which they had mounted into rings.

And Jung was excluded. In June of 1912, he was President of the International Psychoanalytic Society and editor of the *Jahrbuch für psychoanalytische und psychopathologische Forschungen.* He had only begun to broach his different concept of the libido within the last few months, and only openly in two letters to Freud in May. His growing interest in mythology showed that his researches were diverging from most of the other psychoanalysts, but

Freud himself was working with mythology as he prepared his *Totem and Taboo* during this time. Jung's reading of the 'Kreuzlingen gesture' may have been more accurate than it has been thought.

In September, Part Two of *Wandlungen und Symbole der Libido* came out. Part One had appeared in 1911. Both parts were reprinted together in book-form several months later. It was Emma Jung who sent Freud the offprints of Part Two, along with a peace-making note probably designed to explain Jung's long silence:

> Carl was away nearly all summer; since Saturday he has been on the trip to America after spending only one day here between military service and departure. I have so much to do right now that I can't let too much libido travel after him to America, it might so easily get lost on the way.[54]

Apparently, Freud was grateful for this letter.[55] It should be noted that, whether intentionally or not, she was using 'libido' in the Freudian not Jungian sense of the word.

Jung returned from America with the briskness of one who has decided on a new direction, whatever the consequences. The tone of his letters from then until the final break in January 1913 has been called 'truculent,'[56] but it seems instead, decisive. Clearly Jung was allowing himself to put into words what he had been resentfully thinking for a long time. The letters read more like those from someone who has been smarting under the other's power-plays than someone who only wants to smash the other's ego.

Jung's next letter to Freud after his 'Kreuzlingen gesture' letter came in early November when he returned after giving nine lectures on the psychoanalytic movement at the University of Fordham. There, he reported to Freud, he had discussed his own views 'which deviate[d] in places from the hitherto existing conceptions, particularly in regard to the libido theory'. In his letter, Jung again mentioned the 'Kreuzlingen gesture' which gave him 'a lasting wound', but added that he did not want to break off personal relations with Freud. It was simply that he refused 'to be treated like a fool riddled with complexes'.[57]

The reference to Jung's 'complexes' alludes to the long-standing jest between them that the younger man had a 'father-complex' toward Freud. What makes this use of the term at Jung's expense so ironic is that the very concept of the complex was original with Jung, not Freud, yet increasingly in his letters Freud employed it as a weapon against Jung.

Freud's answering letter only included a few brief sarcasms, and was for the most part devoted to business matters. Jung's letter (by return mail, which shows how eagerly he was waiting to hear from Freud) began with a brief defiance – 'I dare not offer you my name for your journal; since you have disavowed me so thoroughly, my collaboration can hardly be acceptable!' – but then ends almost supplicatingly – 'We should not forget that the history of human truths is also the history of human errors. So let us give the well-meant error its rightful place.'[58]

The Munich Conference followed. Freud and Jung met and discussed the 'Kreuzlingen gesture', and it seemed that things were patched over. Back in Zurich, Jung wrote a conciliatory letter asking Freud to 'please forgive the mistakes which I will not try to excuse or extenuate,' and inquired about Freud's health after his long night journey back to Vienna from Munich.[59] For in Munich Freud had had a fainting spell during a conversation with Jung, as he had once before. On both occasions, the two men were in the middle of a spirited discussion on a general topic when Jung said something that Freud took to show a latent hostility; and as a result, Freud fainted.

Freud swiftly replied, with a brutality suggesting that he was only waiting for his opponent to let his guard down. He opened by thanking Jung for his 'friendly letter' that raised 'the best of hopes for our future collaboration,' and said of his fainting spell that it proved to be only a migraine attack with 'a psychic factor' that he had no time to explore, 'a bit of neurosis I really should look into'. (Since he considered it to result from the sudden revelation of Jung's hostility toward him, he could be implying that it was *Jung*'s neurosis.)

He passed to the business matters that occupied the rest of the letter, only slipping into the middle of this neutral subject two poisonous sentences relating to Ferenczi's coming review of Jung's 'libido paper':

> I am gradually coming to terms with this paper (yours, I mean) and I now believe that in it you have brought us a great revelation, though not the one you intended. You seem to have solved the riddle of all mysticism, showing it to be based on the symbolic utilization of complexes that have outlived their function.[60]

These were castrating words. Ostensibly, Freud was recasting Jung's own earlier statements that the true significance of mythology is symbolic (or 'pure fantasy,' as he wrote to Freud) rather than biological or experiential; and again, Freud charged Jung with 'mysticism'. 'Riddle' is of course trivializing also. But Freud's true meaning here was that Jung's concept of the libido was so patently false, that one must see his very attempt to construct it as a sign of mental illness, for it was 'a great revelation' of Jung's father-complex.

Jung took it that way. He opened his next letter by warning Freud that he was writing to him in a new 'style', which turned out to be one of directly expressing his feelings. He picked up Freud's off-handed mention of his own 'neurosis,' commenting that fainting is traditionally a neurotic symptom. Up to this point, Jung had remained silent to Freud about possible conclusions to be drawn from Freud's fainting spells during their conversations, conclusions that might relate more to Freud than to Jung. Jung took up this point again in an openly hostile letter two weeks later.

But now, Jung passed to the wound of Freud's words: everything that Jung thinks or says or writes was reductively psychologized as revealing his 'complexes'. 'A particularly preposterous bit of nonsense now going the rounds is that my libido theory is the product of anal eroticism.' (This is short-hand for Freudian theory about the anal stage of infantile sexuality, the stage preceding the genital stage which prefigures adult experience. The implication is that Freud's theory is the adult experience of sexuality and Jung's is the childish one that has 'retained' mythological materials.) However, Jung wrote, 'I want no infantile outpourings of libidinal appreciation or admiration from psychoanalysts, merely an understanding of my ideas.'[61]

Freud crisply suggested that in the future 'let each of us pay more attention to his own than to his neighbor's neurosis' and then spent the rest of his letter on business, generally implying that Jung was doing a poor job at it. Jung (who had been answering nearly by return mail since his return from the Munich Conference) replied with a letter equally full of business, including a somewhat fawning criticism of Adler's latest book.[62] Freud replied nastily by welcoming this criticism since it 'make[s] for political clarity by putting an end to rumors current here that you are "swinging over" to him'.[63]

Jung replied with one of his few epistolary parapraxes. He meant to write, 'Even Adler's cronies do not regard me as one of theirs', but what he actually wrote was, 'Even Adler's cronies do not regard me as one of yours.'[64] (Fawning is usually self-destructive, and the self can take its own protective measures.) Freud pointed this out to him by return mail, as Jung had not done with Freud's own previous slips of the pen.

Jung answered with fury. 'Your technique of treating your pupils like patients is a *blunder* [italics his]', he began, and went on from there to write of what he saw as Freud's own complex of 'playing the father to your sons and . . . aiming continually at their weak spots'.[65] Freud proved Jung's accuracy by replying drily, 'I am sorry my reference to your slip annoyed you so; your reaction seems out of all proportion to the occasion.'[66]

Letters from Jung and Freud crossed at this point, both dated January 3, 1913. Jung's letter offered Freud his 'friendly wishes for the New Year', and declared that he would write no more 'secret letters' if that was what Freud wished, but that he intended to treat him 'with the same analytical consideration which you extend to me from time to time'.[67] Freud, for his part, 'propose[d] that we abandon our personal relations entirely'.[68]

Jung at once responded: 'I accede to your wish that we abandon our personal relations, for I never thrust my friendship on anyone. You yourself are the best judge of what this moment means to you. "The rest is silence."'[69]

It was finished.

Freud wrote of the taboo and its effects: '"Taboo" . . . is . . . expressed in prohibitions and restrictions. . . . The source of the taboo is attributed to a peculiar magical power which is inherent in persons and spirits.'[70] The characteristic emotional response to the tabooed kept reappearing in these letters by Freud from 1909 through 1912. In them, he instinctively recoiled whenever Jung touched certain areas of thought. He reacted with sarcasm, insults, and parapraxes.

At the same time, his letters showed the process of a taboo being created, for in them he came to define what is 'forbidden'. This act of definition was accompanied by attempts to control Jung, much as the magician casts self-protective spells against the summoned spirits.

One way is through language. Jung's ideas were termed a 'spook-complex', or 'mystical', or 'occult', or 'a fairytale forest feeling', or a 'cloud', all of which were generally interchangeable in their intended meaning. This goes beyond ridicule. Freud was giving Jung a *name,* in the ancient sense of the name that represents the essence of a thing; and his *naming* was done in the spirit of casting a spell.

Similarly, Jung's concept of the libido was dismissed through the language of reductive psychologizing. This can be seen in the persistent allusions to Jung's 'father-complex' that ran through Freud's letters, culminating in his flat statement that Jung's concepts set forth in *Wandlungen und Symbole der Libido* were 'the symbolic utilization of complexes that have outlived their function'. It was revealed also in Jung's remark that according to the current Freudians 'my libido theory is the product of anal eroticism'. This is the fallacy of *argumentum ad hominem,* which was the burden of Jung's futile request that 'I want no infantile outpourings of libidinal appreciation or admiration from psychoanalysts, merely an understanding of my ideas.'

The danger of contagion by the taboo seemed present too. Freud noted:

> Persons or things which are regarded as taboo may be compared to objects charged with electricity; they are the seat of a tremendous power which is transmissible by contact.
>
> The strangest fact seems to be that anyone who has transgressed one of these prohibitions himself acquires the characteristic of being prohibited – as though the whole of the dangerous charge had been transferred over to him.[71]

Fliess's and then Adler's names were invoked in the letters as ominous beings whose presence Jung was approaching. In Fliess's case, it was his betrayal of Freud's friendship by distancing himself that was taboo; while in Adler's case, it was his abandonment of the Freudian concept of the unconscious and theory of libido to emphasize another area of the psyche that was taboo. Jung himself managed to transgress in both ways. The formation of the Secret Committee in June, 1912, showed that the taboo had already begun to 'charge' Jung with a dangerous energy.

This has existed up to the present time. Jung's system of thought is still generally described with the same words that Freud used in his letters. They are not especially precise words, and certainly not terms of discrimination. It is predictable that Freud's championing theorists during the embattled early years of the movement, and then the later orthodox Freudians of the first half of the century, should take Freud's lead here. 'Mystical psychologists' became a kind of code-word for Jung and the Jungians. However, now when the Movement has seemingly become more porous and tolerant of variant schools, whether

Kleinian, Lacanian, or Kohutian, Jung is still being designated in the same way by respected psychoanalytic figures.

Francois Roustang, in a book harshly critical of Freudian orthodoxy, still uses the language of the orthodox to say of Jung that 'he indulges in a formless, mystical doctrine'.[72] Reuben Fine writes in his comprehensive overview of psychoanalysis that Jung 'really should be classified as a religious philosopher'.[73] John Gedo refers to Jung's world of 'occultism', adding that he 'cloaked his mysticism with an empirical veneer'.[74] Peter Gay calls him 'mystical in disposition'.[75] Jay Greenberg and Stephen Mitchell, in their well-received history of object-relations theorists (among whom, as will be seen, are contemporary Jungians whom they omit), sum up Jung's thought as 'a complex and esoteric system of . . . spiritually grounded archetypes'.[76]

This synchronized wording is accompanied by another phenomenon. The taboo surrounding Jung has generally extended to the books he wrote after his 1913 *Symbols of Transformation,* the thirteen volumes of his *Collected Works* in which he worked out his own mature analytic system. Again, this might be expected from the earlier Freudians who closed ranks behind him but not, one would think, from later more inclusive psychologists.

To judge from the accompanying notes and bibliographies of these contemporaries, their main sources of knowledge for their summations of Jung's thought are *Symbols of Transformation,* his autobiography *Memories, Dreams, Reflections,* and/or edited selections of Jung's individual essays. Thus Roustang and Gedo only cite the autobiography; Greenberg and Mitchell, a 1913 essay by Jung. Peter Gay's 'Bibliographical Essay', which again alludes to 'Jung's mysticism',[77] does not make clear which of Jung's *Collected Works* he has read. Fine cites *Symbols of Transformation* and the 1921 *Psychological Types,* neither one of which sets forth Jung's mature theories, and anthologies of Jung's essays by later Jungians.

Often literary critics as well as psychologists write dismissively of Jung's theories, while apparently relying on a knowledge of his work that is second-hand rather than first-hand and seems to derive from Freudians rather than Jung. The 'complex and esoteric system' cited above is, alternately, 'Jung's metaphysic',[78] his 'gendered mysticism',[79] or his 'romantic unconscious'.[80] This last critic reminds us that 'according to Lacan, Freud's concept of reality was probably . . . influenced by Jung's mythic ideas on the evolution of the human spirit'.[81] Greenberg and Mitchell only list in their bibliography one essay by Jung, written in the year of his break with Freud.

It is understandable that those hostile or simply indifferent to Jung because he is forbidden territory for psychoanalysts would not wish to follow the later development of his thought. Who wants to lose face with the experts?

Consider the example of the President of the International Psychoanalytic Association, Robert S. Wallerstein. The subject of his address given to the 1987 International Psychoanalytic Congress was the necessity today for pluralism in psychoanalysis, 'a pluralism of theoretical perspectives'.[82] He admits that 'the Jungian movement . . . has endured worldwide as an alternative therapeutic system' to that of Freud,[83] but then acknowledges that 'I am not myself in a position to have an adequately formed opinion on the psychoanalytic credentials of Jungian theory.'[84] In place of any such first-hand knowledge, he offers the criticisms made by a Jungian analyst of Jung's doctoral dissertation published in 1902 as 'evidence' that Jung's later psychology cannot be considered psychoanalytical.[85] How can there be pluralism if the mature theories of one's 'alternative' opponent are unknown, not considered *worth* knowing?

At the heart of these dismissals of Jung is the satisfied feeling that the exclusion is justified because his method was not based on 'science' as Freud's was. In his own way, however, Jung was working with sciences, for the so-called 'occult' fields of astrology and alchemy were the ancestors of astronomy and chemistry. His method may not have been strictly empirical but it was not really 'mystical', in the sense of seeking realities beyond intellectual comprehension that are accessible to intuition.

Rather he was interested in what those fields could tell him about how the archaic mind worked, and whether the human psyche then might be similar to the human psyche today. Could the archaic psychic insights embodied in those 'occult' fields tell us something about man's psyche that we might not know otherwise? Might these insights illustrate the collective nature of human experience?

But beyond this distortion of Jung's strategy, there is the larger question of whether Freudian psychoanalysis really *is* the science that it claims to be. Freud himself insisted over and over in his essays through the years that it is, following a strictly scientific method of inductive inquiry into human behavior and basing its theories upon observable factual data. This has been an article of faith for later Freudians, whose pride in the 'scientific' and 'empirical' basis of psychoanalysis is well-known. Yet this is precisely the claim that has been under attack for the last several decades by general observers involved in the field, all of them non-Jungians. (The Jungians, of course, have discounted the claim all along.)

Recent studies have come down heavily upon the Freudian insistence that clinical work with patients can provide the evidence that will support psychoanalytic theory. Adolph Grünbaum, in *The Foundations of Psychoanalysis: A Philosophical Critique,* has particularly struck a nerve.[86] This densely written and closely reasoned book sets out to prove that it is impossible to be sure that data from the analytic situation are not the result of suggestion. Nor is there any way to prove its therapeutic value, given its poor (and prolonged) cure rate.

Less technical and more accessible to the general reader is Donald Spence's later work, *The Freudian Metaphor: Toward Paradigm Change in Psychoanalysis.*[87] The Freudian pretensions of employing a method that may accurately be called 'scientific' are definitively dissected, as Spence shows how genuine sciences are objective disciplines open to all comers while psychoanalysis has always been a self-referential, closed discourse.[88] He demonstrates the ways in which the theories of psychoanalysis are based upon metaphors of the mind that are empirically unprovable.

There are also critiques that hit closer to home. For nearly a decade, the accuracy of the James Strachey translation has been challenged. Was Freud as 'scientific' as he seemed to be to the reader of the English *Standard Edition*? Was the translation by James Strachey deliberately engineered to produce through style and rhetoric the impression that psychoanalysis is indeed a science? The issue goes deeper than literary or even psychoanalytic accuracy, however. The events surrounding the translation of Freud's German works again show the drive towards an orthodoxy that excluded anything touching upon the tabooed territory of 'occultism' or 'mysticism'.

A. A. Brill was Freud's first translator, producing an English version of *The Interpretation of Dreams* in 1913 as part of his enthusiastic missionary activities on behalf of Freud to the United States. He and Ernest Jones planned a literal translation of Freud, and Jones assumed to himself (with the tacit approval of all) the authority to control the translation and designate the translator.[89] Jones himself continued to translate Freud's essays between 1913 and 1923. He introduced distinctly technical terminology into the psychoanalytic discourse such as 'ego ideal,' 'parapraxis,' and probably 'anaclitic,' as well as full terminological glossaries. Jones favored terms with ancient Greek and Latin roots, and to an extent 'standardized' Freud's writing by using these terms in the English version.[90] Jones and other closely connected collaborators continued their translatings through the 1920s.

Among these collaborators was the British James Strachey, who had worked on the project since the earliest days. He had helped to produce the first comprehensive Glossary, introducing the famous term 'cathexis', and many other technical terms. He too favored a translation marked by words and terms stemming from ancient Greek and Latin, for this suggested a medical and thus an empirical basis to Freud's writings.

Freud generally assented to the translations, the technical terminology, and the glossaries. But all of these were done several years, sometimes decades, after the composition of Freud's essays. By then the discourse had crystallized, both for the Freudians and for Freud. Nor was a hindsight revisionism on Freud's part unlikely.

He supported Strachey as the official translator, and later his redoubtable daughter Anna Freud gave her full support to the veracity of Strachey's translation. For the next few decades Strachey persevered in this formidable task that called for much time and energy, reworking the translations of others and 'standardizing' Freud's literary style.[91]

The result was the *Standard Edition* published between 1955 and 1967, which has proved to be the only source for most American and British readers of Freud. Relatively few of these readers know German, or Freud's frequently idiomatic Viennese German, well enough to read Freud himself.

Certainly translating Freud's works was an enormous undertaking, and not only because of the number of essays that Freud wrote or the difficulties of translating his sometimes idiomatic German style. Quite often Freud was inventing the term that best captured a theoretical concept original with him, so that in a peculiar way the word *was* the meaning without any semantic precedent for the translator to fall back on. There are not many today who would care to re-translate the *Standard Edition*. But dissatisfactions with it have increasingly been sounded. One recent proposal by a German analyst has been to publish an edition with three texts side by side: Freud's German one, Strachey's translation, and a commentary that allows for different possible readings.[92]

The Freudian analyst Bruno Bettelheim was brought up in Freud's Vienna, and thus uniquely understood the flavor of Freud's German text. In *Freud and Man's Soul*, he details the extent to which Freud relied upon the humanist tradition for his metaphors, allusions, and key words chosen to designate his theories (such as Oedipal complex).[93] A prime example of the changes made by Jones and then Strachey is their translation of Freud's frequently used word 'Seele', or soul, as psyche. 'Psyche' may be the Greek word for soul, but in its connotations it means more narrowly the mind functioning as the center of thoughts, feelings, and behavior. There are religious overtones to the word 'soul' that there are not to 'psyche'.

More recently, the psychiatrist Darius Ornston, Jr, in criticizing Strachey's *Standard Edition* charges that 'Freud's own imaginative pictures of unconscious life are much more variegated than Strachey's. . . Strachey simplifies.'[94] That is, Freud uses metaphors and imagery from many fields besides nineteenth-century biology.

Thus Freud may be closer in his style and rhetoric to Jung than his English readers suspect, as his own interests in telepathy and the 'uncanny' were closer than he wanted to acknowledge. What Jones and Strachey, and the 'Committee' backing them, excluded was that which seemed 'unscientific'– in fact, that which seemed close to the tabooed voice.

In the official publication of the International Psychoanalytic Association, the Freudian analyst Emmett Wilson attacks all those who would consider that Strachey's translation ignored Freud's humanist side. The old familiar anathemas are employed: such critics are 'spiritualists' and 'soulful revisionists'.[95] After all, Wilson adds, Strachey's translation was not meant to replace Freud since the reader can always go to Freud himself – a disingenuous argument, given the linguistic demands this makes upon the reader.

In any case, Wilson continues, an important issue to be considered must be that the International Psychoanalytical Association uses Strachey's *Standard Edition* as a source of income – and so 'the Society would of course want to retain control of [any new translations]'.[96]

2

Appropriation

Marginalizing may also be accomplished through appropriation. The ideas which are original with the figure being marginalized, but fruitful anyway, are co-opted so that the source of the ideas seems to be the central figure rather than the marginal one. Thus it comes to seem, to all save the marginal who has been looted, that the central figure deserves its position.

This need not be a deliberate, planned process. If one begins with the assumption that the marginal figure *by nature* can have nothing to do with one's discourse, then it becomes plausible to deny that the marginal could have anything to contribute to it. If what this marginal figure *is* defines that which the discourse is *not,* then there really cannot be any similarities between the two. Determination of orthodoxy becomes that much clearer and easier. Such co-option is control at the source. To appropriate is to redefine.

The letters between Jung and Freud reveal something of this process. The letters are a particularly valuable window into each at this point, for each was struggling to formulate his thought: Jung, what his was, and Freud, what his was not. The appropriation occurred in the field of mythology, exactly the area to which Jung was devoting so much enthusiastic energy and exactly the area in which he was threatening to break away with his own line of thought.

As the letters progress, one sees simultaneously Freud's co-opting of Jung's explorations in mythology and Jung's increasing reluctance to share his ideas on the subject with Freud. This was likely due in part to Jung's awareness as his ideas took shape that they pointed toward an inevitable break with Freud's theories. But the reluctance probably had a more practical base as well: Jung feared Freud's pre-emption. It was not simply a matter of possible plagiarism by Freud, although that did enter into it. It was rather that Freud attempted to control signs of independence, or even the desire for independence – as Jung seemed to recognize.

In late 1909, Jung began writing to Freud about his discoveries in ancient Classical and Eastern mythology. He had been studying the field for some time before this, but evidently had not felt enough in control of the materials or his interpretations of them to write much to Freud about the subject. In October he wrote, predicting what turned out to be true of his future work: 'I am obsessed by the thought of one day writing a comprehensive account of this whole field, after years of fact-finding and preparation, of course. The net should be cast wide. Archaeology or rather mythology has got me in its grip, it's a mine of marvelous material.'[1]

Freud answered immediately, giving general news and sounding the first note of an appropriation that grew louder and louder in his letters to Jung as Freud re-stated what Jung had first said in such a way that it sounded Freudian: 'I am glad that you share my belief that we must conquer the whole field of mythology. [Jung had expressed the "belief" that he, not "we", would track this field.] Thus far we have only two pioneers: Abraham and Rank [two of the most stalwart of the faithful around Freud then]. We need men for more far-reaching campaigns.'[2]

This produced a hiatus of three weeks in the correspondence. Then Jung wrote again in some detail of his rather esoteric researches into Greek mythology – to stress that he was not one of the militia? 'One of the reasons why I didn't write for so long is that I was immersed every evening . . . in mythology and archaeology. I have been reading Herodotus. . . . Now I am reading the 4 volumes of old Creuzer, where there is a huge mass of material.'[3] He unfolded before Freud the theory of myth he had reached, showing that he was indeed on his own solitary campaign. The ideas advanced in his letters of November 8 and 15

1909, and then in that of January 30 1910, were rudimentary but recognizable versions of his later theories of the collective unconscious and the archetypes. In his November 8 letter he wrote: 'All my delight in archaeology [Jung's term for his excavations into ancient mythologies] (buried for years) has sprung to life again. Rich lodes open up for the phylogenetic basis of neurosis.'[4]

Phylogeny is the evolutionary development of a species of plant or animal. Jung proposes here that neurosis has a universal, and not merely an individual, pattern of development, and further, that this pattern may be discerned in ancient mythology . Ancient mythology thus may symbolize man's psychological experiences that are still as true today as they were in archaic times. The study of ancient mythology may help us understand contemporary neurosis.

Freud answered the day he got this letter, opening with an allusion to Fliess:

> It probably isn't nice of you to keep me waiting 25 days (from October 14 to November 8; I checked because I suspected one of Fliess's 23-day periods, but wrong again) for an answer – as though the promptness and length [but not the contents?] of my last letter had frightened you away.[5]

Then came a significant parapraxis, as Freud wrote of his Viennese followers: 'I wish you had a single backside so that I could thrash them all with a single stick,' when he intended to write 'I wish *they* had a single backside.'[6]

There followed more appropriation: 'I was delighted to learn that you are going into mythology. A little less loneliness [implying thus that Freud himself was first in the territory]. I can't wait to learn of your discoveries.' Then came the reminder that Freud himself had already thought of the 'likelihood' of these ideas that Jung was developing laboriously by studying the original sources: 'I hope you will soon come to agree with me that in all likelihood mythology centers on the same nuclear complex as the neuroses.' In fact, Freud suggests, this theory is so obvious that it has occurred not only to doctors and former university professors such as themselves, but to Gymnasium teachers (the European equivalent of American high school teachers): 'Recently chance brought me a young Gymnasium teacher who is studying mythology. His ideas are similar to *ours*' [italics mine].[7]

However, Jung had not really been proposing what Freud said he was proposing. By 'nuclear complex,' Freud meant the Oedipal complex centering around the infantile desire for incest. But Jung did not consider this to be the only 'phylogenetic basis of neurosis,' as became clearer in subsequent letters. He had in mind something more audacious.

In his answering letter of November 15, Jung took up Freud's phrase 'nuclear complex' with a flourish. He agreed that ancient myths 'speak quite "naturally" of the nuclear complex of neurosis', detailing an example from Herodotus of a festival for the mother of Ares which illustrated the Oedipal conflict. Then he passed to examples from other Greek and Near Eastern cults in which the gods being worshipped were 'everywhere phallic'.[8] He concluded that the great difficulty he was encountering was dating the widely spread myths to determine which were genuine and which merely literary derivatives, a problem that he noted is typically known by the ethnologist although unimportant to the philologist.[9]

This letter might seem to agree with Freud's statement about the 'nuclear complex [of] the neuroses', particularly since Jung uses the same phrase. But there was a subtle yet real distinction that Jung was making between what Freud meant and what he meant. He began with an example of a festival that was obviously 'Oedipal' in the Freudian sense, and then went on to cite several cults whose gods were 'everywhere phallic'. This implied that the infantile incestuous desire for the mother is not the sole 'nuclear complex,' and that ancient mythology symbolized other psychic truths as well. Moreover, the cults that Jung mentioned are not merely the usual Greek ones familiar to most educated Europeans then, but those of Thrace, Phrygia, Babylon, and Egypt. Terming himself an ethnologist, rather than merely a philologist, was a way of stressing the rigorous nature of his own specialized researches.

All of this answered the condescension running just under the surface of Freud's letter: with Jung showing how much more comprehensive is his own grasp of the material than any 'young Gymnasium teacher', emphasizing that his theories are not based on the speculation of 'likelihood' but on extensive research, and suggesting that the Oedipal complex is not the only neurosis to be symbolized in ancient mythology.

On and on it went in their letters of this period, as Jung would posit some new idea based on mythology and Freud would swiftly appropriate it through re-statement.

In answer to Jung's November 15 letter, Freud declared himself 'delighted with your mythological studies'. He wrote, concerning Jung's mention of the festivals surrounding the cult of Cybele and of the 'phallic' gods Adonis, Osiris, Orpheus, and Tammuz: 'Much of what you write is quite new to me, e.g., the mother-lust, the idea that priests emasculated themselves to punish themselves for it' – not at all what Jung did write. And then he translated the cults that Jung has been studying: they all illustrate 'the castration complex in myth'.[10]

Jung stubbornly returned to the insight of his November 8 letter, elaborating on his gnomic statement that mythology is 'the phylogenetic basis of the theory of neurosis'.[11] On December 2, 1909, Jung wrote:

> I feel more and more that a thorough understanding of the psyche (if possible at all) will only come through history or with its help. Just as an understanding of anatomy and ontogenesis is possible only on the basis of phylogenesis and comparative anatomy. What we now find in the individual psyche – in compressed, stunted, or one-sided differentiated form – may be seen spread out in all its fullness in times past.[12]

This was the germ of his later theory of the collective unconscious.

Freud responded: 'Apropos of mythology: have you observed that the sexual theories of children are indispensable for the understanding of myth?'[13] He added tartly: 'I believe that [after my retirement] the younger men will demolish everything in my heritage that is not absolutely solid as fast as they can . . . . Since you are likely to play a prominent part in this work of liquidation, I shall try to place certain of my endangered ideas in your safekeeping.'[14] The 'idea' then discussed at length was his concept of the libido.

Jung replied within a few days in a way suggesting that perhaps he was not the best guardian for the estate.

> But most of all I was struck by your remark that you longed for archaeologists, philologists, etc. By this, I told myself, you probably meant that I was unfit for such work. However, it is in precisely those fields that I now have a passionate interest. . . . And I have the most marvelous visions, glimpses of far-reaching interconnections which I am at present incapable of grasping . . . . It has become quite clear to me that we shall not solve the ultimate secrets of neurosis and psychosis without mythology and the history of civilization.[15]

He added a postscript to this letter a few days later before posting it, that specifically contradicted Freud's remark about 'the sexual theories of children' explaining ancient myth.

> I am turning over and over in my mind the problem of antiquity. . . . it seems to me that there's a lot of infantile sexuality in it, but that is not all. Rather it seems to me that antiquity was ravaged by the struggle with *incest,* with which sexual *repression* begins (or is it the other way round?) [italics his].[16]

'The other way round' is a distinctly non-Freudian idea, for Freud would have said that it is the 'struggle with incest' that always causes the 'sexual repression'.

Promptly, Freud rejoiced:

> Your displeasure at my longing for an army of philosophical collaborators is music to my ears. I am delighted that you yourself take this interest so seriously, that you yourself wish to be in this army; I could have dreamed of nothing better but simply did not suspect that mythology and archaeology has taken such a powerful hold on you. But I must have hoped as much, for since October something has diverted me from working in those fields. . . . But may I confide a source of misgiving? I don't think it would be a good idea to plunge directly into the general problem of ancient mythology; it strikes me as preferable to approach it in a series of detailed studies. . . . What I have valued in the specialists was simply the sheer knowledge that is so hard for us to acquire.[17]

In other words, Jung was to do the spadework for the one who will supply the theory.

The 'something' that had kept Freud from working in the fields of mythology and archaeology was his study of contemporary anthropology that would lead to his 1913 work, *Totem and Taboo.* Freud had begun working on this in early 1910,[18] and continued through 1911 as he reviewed the technical literature in the field. But by 1911 he already had his general theory in mind, for, as he wrote to Ferenczi, he was 'reading fat books without real interest, since I already know the results'.[19] In early February 1912, the connection between totemism and ambivalence suddenly fell into place for him, and he began writing the essays that comprised *Totem and Taboo.*[20]

Jung's letter of January 10, 1910, sounded the first tentative note of reserve at sharing his discoveries and ideas so freely with Freud: 'Mythology certainly has me in its grip. I bring to it a good deal of archaeological interest from my early days. I don't want to say too much now but would rather wait for it to ripen.'[21]

Three weeks later, Jung wrote about two public lectures that he had just given as part of a series of six he was presenting on mental illness in childhood. They evidently were a significant formulation for him of his theories so far, for the ones on symbolism became an early draft of *Wandlungen und Symbole der Libido.*[22] They extended his earlier ideas on the 'phylogenetic basis of neurosis,' and even more clearly pointed to his later theory of the collective unconscious. He wrote to Freud: 'I . . . have tried to put the 'symbolic' on a psychogenetic foundation, i.e., to show that in the individual fantasy the *primum movens,* the individual conflict, is mythic, or mythologically typical. The supporting material is rather thin.'[23] He did not supply any of the 'supporting material'.

He did not write much about mythological matters for the next few months. On March 2, 1910, he wrote, in answer to a letter from Freud that is unfortunately missing: 'Your conception of the ucs. [the unconscious] . . . is in striking agreement with what I said in my January lecture on symbolism.'[24]

He would seem to be simply noting a similarity. Put together with other comments in their letters around this time, it may also point to a growing uneasiness that he wished to put into words.

Throughout this time, Jung was engrossed in writing the heavily mythological *Wandlungen.* On May 24, 1910, he wrote to Freud that he had just given another public lecture on symbolism with 'mythological stuff,' and was sending a copy of it to Freud.[25] Freud at once replied that he would be 'delighted' to get it, 'especially as I am counting on your formulations to clarify certain vague ideas of my own'.[26] Jung answered, 'My mythology swirls around inside me, and now and then various significant bits and pieces are thrown up.'[27] Then he specified some of the 'bits and pieces,' all of which related to incest and the libido. Freud's answering letter closed by indicating that he was 'eagerly waiting your mythology'.[28]

Jung sent his January lecture on symbolism for Freud to read. This was a very early draft of *Wandlungen,* now missing so that one cannot tell exactly what Freud read, but it must have been plain to him that Jung's concept of the libido was not his own. Freud sent back his critique of it, particularly objecting to Jung's statement, 'Sexuality destroys itself', as explaining the mythological motif of self-sacrifice. The castration complex, Freud thought, was much the more obvious motivation for the motif.

Near the end of this critique, Freud added two curious sentences:

> Don't be surprised if you recognize certain of your statements in a paper of mine that I am hoping to revise in the first weeks of the holidays, and don't accuse me of plagiarism, though there may be some temptation to. . . . I conceived and wrote it before the arrival of your 'Symbolism': it is of course a formulation of ideas that were long present in my mind.[29]

The obvious question to be asked of Freud here was why, if he thought he might be at all guilty of plagiarizing, he did not simply ascribe those ideas not his own to the correct source through citations or, at least acknowledge that his correspondent had just reached similar conclusions – and given public lectures on them, too.

Jung immediately replied to Freud's criticisms at length, particularly Freud's comment that 'the whole thing should not really be titled 'Symbolism', but 'Symbolism and Mythology', since more light is thrown on the latter than the former.'[30] Jung made it clear that for him the two subjects were not discrete, since he thought that ancient mythology revealed the symbols of the libido that man still experiences today: that there is a collective substratum of experience shared by past and present mankind, in other words. Several sentences announce distinctly non-Freudian concerns, as when he alludes to the prototypical hero who 'realize[s] the ethical ideal of the subjugation of instinct'[31] and the hero's necessary self-sacrifice being due to the 'force compelling him towards culture'.[32]

Jung did not comment directly about Freud's attempt to forestall the charge of plagiarism. However he showed a protective memory-lapse of his own, for he began his answering letter by mentioning that the copyist had left out a key passage on self-sacrifice (presumably having to do with symbolic or literal castration in some way) and that 'the discussion of the incest problem is also missing'.[33] But he did not supply the omissions.

He did defend his statement that 'sexuality destroys itself', for it went to the heart of his differences with Freud on the nature of the libido. Freud's suggestion that the self-sacrifice motif points to the castration complex is 'admittedly [a] much simpler explanation,' but Jung has in mind something more complex: 'a conflict at the heart of sexuality itself'. This conflict can only be due to 'the incest prohibition [that] blocks the nearest and most convenient outlet for the libido and makes it altogether bad'. The 'conflict' itself was necessary 'in order to realize the ethical ideal of the subjugation of instinct'.[34] These attempts by man at 'self subjugation' in ancient mythology symbolized 'the force compelling him towards culture'.[35]

All of this is quite different from Freud's concept of the libido and his theories of the primary role of repression in the formation of neuroses – at that time. It is notably similar to Freud's later ideas expressed in *Civilization and its Discontents.* This is *not* to suggest any conscious influence or unconscious borrowing in that work. It is only to point out that later theories of Freud generally accepted by those in the mainstream of the psychoanalytic discourse had had their earlier, extended expression in the *Wandlungen* of the marginalized Jung.

Jung did not write again about his mythological studies until December 1910, and then only in very general words. By then he had finished Part One of *Wandlungen.* Although he was to visit Freud in Munich over the holidays, he did not bring any part of the manuscript for him to read, saying that it still had to be copied out. He warned: 'But be prepared for some strange things the like of which you have never heard from me,'[36] again without giving specifics. In January, 1911, he noted that Part One was still being copied out and thus unavailable for Freud to read.[37] Jung never did show the manuscript to Freud. Part One of *Wandlungen* was first published on August 20, 1911, as a long article in *Jahrbuch,* Volume III:1.

Freud responded characteristically to Jung's January refusal to send on Part One. His answering letter included a long paragraph about Adler's current mistaken theory that 'the motivation . . . of coitus was not exclusively sexual', thus bracketing Jung and his emerging libido theory with the dismissed Adler. Then he ended with the information that

> yesterday I received a little essay on the cult of Mithras by Kluge. . . . I don't know why you are so afraid of my criticism in matters of mythology. I shall be very happy when you plant the flag of libido and repression in that field and return as a victorious conqueror to our medical motherland.[38]

This efficiently suggested that Jung was only one of many philologists working with the same materials, reminded Jung that psychoanalysis could only be based on 'medical' knowledge, and appropriated all that Jung might have to say about 'libido and repression'.

Jung did not discuss mythology again for five months. Then he returned to the subject, using Freud's earlier metaphor to state his own different, non-medical readings of mythology: 'Occultism is another field we shall have to conquer – with the aid of the libido theory, it seems to me. At the moment, I am looking into astrology, which seems indispensable for a proper understanding of mythology.' Then there were a few vague sentences about the 'magic perfumes' of the unconscious realms he was exploring and the 'rich booty' that he would bring back, although again he gave no specifics.

Predictably, Freud replied that Jung would 'be accused of mysticism'.[39] In June, 1911, Jung noted (in the middle of a letter filled with business details) that his evenings were taken up with the study of astrology, and he was beginning to use it as part of his clinical method with promising results.[40] Freud's answer was that he would withhold comment until Jung published his discoveries.[41]

Freud had always had a general interest in mythology and classical Greek culture, due in part to his own personal inclination as well as to his background as an educated European. Allusions to classical mythology ran through his writings, and he often used examples from it to elucidate his analytic theories. But about this time, he began a more intensive study of mythology. He announced this to Jung in late August, 1911, writing:

> Since my mental powers revived [presumably a reference to the refreshment of his recent summer holidays], I have been working in a field where you will be surprised to meet me. I have unearthed strange and uncanny things and almost feel obliged *not* to discuss them with you. But you are too shrewd not to guess what I am up to when I add that I am dying to read your 'Transformations and Symb. of the Lib' [*Wandlungen*].[42]

This letter by Freud was written on the day that the *Jahrbuch* appeared containing Part One of *Wandlungen.* Thus Part One had been withheld from him by Jung until it had been publicly attributed to Jung. The 'field' where Freud had been 'working' was the research for *Totem and Taboo.*

Jung's immediate uneasiness was clear in his next letter.

> Your letter has got me on tenterhooks because, for all my 'shrewdness', I can't quite make out what is going on so enigmatically behind the scenes. Together with my wife I have tried to unriddle your words, and we have reached surmises which, for the time being at any rate, I would rather keep to myself.[43]

Freud expansively enlightened him by return mail. By this time, he had read the *Jahrbuch* volume.

> I am glad to release you as well as your dear wife . . . from the darkness by informing you that my work in these last few weeks has dealt with the same theme as yours, to wit, the origin of religion. But since I can see from a first reading of your article in *Jahrbuch* . . .that my conclusions are known to you, I find, much to my relief, that there is no need for secrecy. So you too are aware that the Oedipus complex is at the heart of religious

> feeling. [The letters that Jung had written to him, and certainly Part One of *Wandlungen*, suggested that this was not Jung's belief.] Bravo! What evidence I have to contribute can be told in five minutes.[44]

Here the Third Psychoanalytic Congress at Weimar intervened. Freud and Jung were among those reading papers. Freud's included this sentence: '[These remarks] may serve to show that Jung had excellent grounds for his assertion that the mythopoeic forces of mankind are not extinct, but that to this very day they give rise in the neuroses to the same psychical products as in the remotest past ages.'[45] Jung's paper on symbolism has not survived, but it seems to have contained material used in Part Two of *Wandlungen*. Then Jung spent several weeks on his annual military duty.

While he was there, Freud sent him a letter that continued conversations they had had on the psychoanalytic meaning of the Gilgamesh myth. He concluded with this sentence: 'If there is such a thing as a phylogenetic memory in the individual, which unfortunately soon will be undeniable, this is also the source of the uncanny aspect of the "doppelgänger".'[46] This is a revealing sentence.

Jung had first proposed that the individual possesses a 'phylogenetic memory,' as we can see from his earlier letters. Here, the source of 'such a thing' is not cited, as if the idea had been absorbed into the body of psychoanalysis to the extent that Freud himself was using it to explain the Gilgamesh myth.

In hindsight, we can see that Freud is casting forward to his 1919 essay 'The Uncanny', where he discusses the doppelgänger and the true source of man's sense of 'the uncanny'– which turns out to be the 'phylogenetic memory' of the maternal genitals. However, this essay is usually considered to be anything but Jungian.

This 'phylogenetic memory in the individual' became Jung's later 'collective unconscious', the part of his analytic theory that to later Freudians has most marginalized him. Yet here Freud was reluctantly ('unfortunately') admitting that it is 'undeniable'.

Jung wrote back from the barracks at once, pleased that Freud seemed to support his theory. He gave a few further examples in support of the idea that some early childhood memories are not individual ones but 'phylogenetic memories'.[47] Freud seemed to be allowing more theoretical leeway than earlier.

However, the full scope of the situation became more apparent with a letter from Freud in November, 1911, commenting on *Wandlungen.*

> The reading for my psychology of religion is going slowly. One of the nicest works I have read (again), is that of a well-known author on the 'Transformations and Symbols of the Libido'. In it many things are so well-expressed that they seem to have taken on definitive form and in this form impress themselves on the memory. . . . Not least, I am delighted by the many points of agreement with things I have already said or would like to say. Since you yourself are this author, I shall continue more directly and make an admission: it is a torment to me to think, when I conceive an idea now and then, that I may be taking something away from you or appropriating something that might just as well have been acquired by you. . . . Why in God's name did I allow myself to follow you into this field? . . . But probably my tunnels will be far more subterranean than your shafts and we shall pass each other by, but every time I rise to the surface I shall be able to greet you.[48]

This letter made it clear that other dynamics were operating than merely a fruitful interchange of ideas between two intellectual friends who were coincidentally researching the same field.

Jung's letters for the past two years had made it plain how deeply involved he had become in the study of ancient mythology. Through it, he was branching off into areas of inquiry that were far afield from Freudian analytic theory. He had written freely to Freud during those past years about his discoveries regarding 'the psychogenetic origin of the neuroses' and 'the phylogenetic memory in the individual', and possible ways in which ancient mythology may symbolize infantile conflicts still experienced by contemporary man. He had given many public lectures on these subjects as well. He was just finishing a long, densely detailed manuscript on the psychoanalytic meaning of the symbolism of mythology, a book that was intended to be his own original and non-Freudian contribution to psychoanalysis.

Freud's own general interest in mythology suddenly quickened near the end of Jung's process of exploration, and four months earlier he had begun close research into the field of mythology in preparation for a new book of his own on the subject, *Totem and Taboo.* The language of his November letter just quoted implies that Jung has done the preliminary work that Freud is now finishing: 'I am delighted [by *Wandlungen*'s] . . . many points of agreement with things I have already said or *would like to say*' [italics added]. Jung's ideas are thus appropriated at the source, Freud's own even before Freud has said them! Not only that, but Freud's own work, just begun a few months ago, is already far more 'subterranean' and thus in tune with depth psychology, than Jung's own thinking of many years on the subject.

The matter went deeper than an appropriation by Freud of Jung's ideas, although Jung's earlier ideas do resurface in *Totem and Taboo.* It is more that Freud's sudden desire to research and write *Totem and Taboo* seems primarily motivated by the desire to deny – even to prevent – Jung's independence by pre-empting his territory of mythology. The whole situation here between Freud and Jung was reminiscent of the earlier one between Freud and Fliess.

By 1904 the deep friendship between Fliess and Freud had definitely waned, but its last blow came when Fliess accused Freud (rightfully, it seems) of having passed along his ideas on bisexuality to others without attributing them to Fliess. What made it worse was that one of Freud's former patients, Swoboda, passed these ideas to another person, who published a book setting forth these ideas as his own.[49]

A week later, after Freud's answering letter mentioning that 'bisexuality comes up for discussion in every treatment',[50] Fliess added:

> Until now I did not know what I learned from your letter – that you are using [the idea of] persistent bisexuality in your treatments. We talked about it for the first time in Nuremberg. . . . At the time you were quite impressed by the idea that undercurrents in a woman might stem from the masculine part of her psyche. For this reason I was all the more puzzled by your resistance in Breslau to the assumption of bisexuality in the psyche.[51]

In other words, Freud's ideas on bisexuality had not occurred to him independently of Fliess.

Freud's answering letter admitted Fliess's charges, but denied much guilt. He took the same line as he did later with Jung: useful ideas 'belong' to no-one.

> I see that I have to concede to you more right than I was originally prepared to . . . I was also quite alarmed by the chapter on hysteria [by Weininger] . . . and I must have regretted at the time that via Swoboda, as I already knew, I had handed over your idea to him . . . [But] ideas can not be patented. One can withhold them – and does so advisedly if one sets great store by one's right of ownership. Once they have been let loose, they go their own way.[52]

Freud thus reminded Fliess that he too had had his theories on hysteria used by Weininger (although Freud's work on hysteria was well-known whereas Fliess's on bisexuality was not). Freud also shifted the blame to Fliess for not withholding his ideas in the first place. But still, intellectual honesty usually calls for the correct attribution of ideas not one's own if one uses them.

Jung's reply to Freud, in November 1911, showed that he took Freud's announcement that he was 'follow[ing Jung] into this field' as pre-emption. He wrote by return mail:

> The outlook for me is very gloomy if you too get into the psychology of religion. You are a dangerous rival – if one has to speak of rivalry . . . Naturally you will be ahead of me in certain respects, but this won't matter much since you have anticipated by far the greatest part already. It is difficult only at first to accustom oneself to this thought. Later one comes to accept it.'[53]

Freud wrote again on the subject two weeks later, writing that he was having difficulties in his work on totemism. 'I don't know yet if I shall be able to float my craft again. In all events it is going very slowly and time alone will prevent us from colliding or crashing.'[54] And then he spelled out explicitly the point on which they were going to 'collide,' thus evidently one reason he was writing the work: as another substantiation of his libido theory. Freud had written two years ago that it was necessary to 'conquer the whole field of mythology', and that although Abraham and Rank had already begun to do this 'we need men for more far-reaching campaigns'.[55] Apparently, he had decided that the job had better be done by himself, and quickly.

In early January, 1912, Freud informed Jung that *Imago,* the new journal he was helping to found, would contain three of his essays on 'the analogies between the psychology of primitive peoples and that of neurotics'.[56] These were the essays on totemism that he had been working on for the last five months, and together with a fourth essay they became *Totem and Taboo.* Two weeks later, he announced that this issue of *Imago* would be printed on February 1. Jung did not immediately reply, and when he did he mentioned that he was in the middle of struggling with 'the hydra of mythological fantasy',[57] a reminder that he was continuing to work on *Wandlungen.* Freud at once responded with his comment that in so doing Jung was 'hid[ing] behind [his] religious-libidinal cloud'.[58]

Jung answered by thanking him for the two *Imago*-destined articles he had just sent, since 'I say quite a lot about [their subject] in Part II of my work on libido, which by the way has taken on alarming proportions.'[59] A week later Jung followed up with a clearer statement of what would appear in that Part II: 'all the problems that arise out of the mother-incest libido, or rather, the libido-cathected mother-imago'.[60] Very succinctly, Jung thus disposed of Freud's Oedipal theory (and thus his libido-theory) in four words. It is not necessarily an actual mother that has caused the infantile neurosis, but an 'imago' of the mother that has been 'cathected' by the libido – a libido that presumably cathects other 'imagos' as well and thus does not derive solely from the actual infantile experience of the mother.

Freud's letter in reply noted that he was just finishing his paper on taboo for *Imago* to accompany those on totemism, and that the journal itself was to appear sometime in March. The letters between Freud and Jung from March onward entered their final, most rancorous stage.

Freud thus was publishing his own fairly brief essays on the 'phylogenetic memory in the individual' and the 'psychogenetic basis of neurosis' about six months after beginning to write them. Three of them were to appear as a substantial part of the first issue of a journal he himself was founding, and thus were guaranteed rapid publication. This was done while Jung was just finishing a three-hundred-page manuscript on the same subject, that he had been working on for at least two years. Freud's actions revealed swiftness in reaching theoretical conclusions ('my interest [in totemism] is diminished by the conviction that I am already in possession of the truths I am trying to prove', he wrote in December, 1911)[61] and haste in trying to get his own essays into print first.

The published *Totem and Taboo* finished this process of appropriation, if not pre-emption. It appeared about a year after Freud's break with Jung, and its Preface reflects some of the after-effects of this break in its dismissal of 'the Zurich school of psychoanalysis'. (Henceforth, Jungians were not usually named by Freudians but rather became 'the Zurich school,' when mentioned at all.) Still, the Preface is telling when juxtaposed with the first two essays, which were the papers *Imago* published in March, 1912.

These essays were intended as 'a methodological contrast' to 'the Zurich school' although, Freud then admits, that school was one of the sources that gave him 'the first stimulus for [his] own essays'. Nevertheless, his essays constitute the 'pioneering work' in the field, for their aim is to 'seek to bridge the gap between students of such subjects as social anthropology, philology, and folklore on the one hand, and psycho-analysis on the other'.[62] The clear implication is that while 'the Zurich school' whetted his interest in the subject, it was Freud who first sought to extend psychoanalysis to these other areas.

Freud in his Preface may have claimed that *Totem and Taboo* was the 'pioneering work', although its stimulus came from Jung (whose *Wandlungen* is cited by publication date, not name); and he might also have implied that since his essays were published 'earlier' in a periodical, they predated *Wandlungen* (although Part One of Jung's book had actually been published in 1911). It might seem that there is a considerable difference between the ancient esoteric mythologies of *Wandlungen,* and the contemporary 'social anthropology' of *Totem and Taboo.* But the general theory underlying the mythological and anthropological specifics of the two books is similar, and it was first fully articulated by Jung: in earlier letters to Freud, in public lectures, and in Part One of *Wandlungen* that had appeared in *Jahrbuch.*

Jung had written in November 1909, that his study of mythology pointed to 'the phylogenetic basis of neurosis',[63] and elaborated on this in December: 'A thorough understanding of the psyche . . . will only come through history or with its help. . . . What we now find in the individual psyche – in compressed, stunted, or one-sided differentiated form – may be seen spread out in all its fullness in times past.'[64] A month later, he added: 'I . . . have tried to put the 'symbolic' on a psychogenetic foundation, i.e., to show that in the individual fantasy the *primum movens,* the individual conflict, is mythic, or mythologically typical.'[65]

In content and spirit, this is close to the opening sentences of Freud's *Totem and Taboo.* Freud, too, sees 'prehistoric man' as being 'still our contemporary'. Rather than going to ancient mythology for proof, however, Freud has chosen to consider

> men still living who . . . stand very near to primitive man . . . Such is our view of those whom we describe as savages or half-savages; and their mental life must have a peculiar interest for us if we are right in seeing in it a well-preserved picture of an early stage of our own development . . . [Thus] a comparison between the psychology of primitive peoples . . . and the psychology of neurotics, as it has been revealed by psycho-analysis, will be bound to show numerous points of agreement and will throw new light upon familiar facts in both sciences.[66]

There were several places in *Totem and Taboo* where Freud drew even nearer to Jung. Twice he echoed Jung's insight about 'the phylogenetic basis of neurosis' in ways that anticipated Jung's later full-blown theory that all men share a collective unconscious as a sub-stratum to the individual personal unconscious. It is startling to read these sentences by Freud proposing that which later most marginalized Jung from the discourse.

Thus Freud, on taboo prohibitions: '. . . in later generations they may have become "organized" as an inherited psychic endowment. Who can decide whether such things as "innate ideas" exist?'[67] And later, after a discussion of the ambivalence that surrounds taboos for primitive peoples, he wrote: 'Neurotics, who are obliged to reproduce the struggle and the taboo resulting from it, may be said to have inherited an archaic constitution as an atavistic vestige.'[68]

Freud's language was plainer than Jung's, and his illustrations from 'social anthropology' far less profuse than Jung's from mythology in *Wandlungen* (though no less academic, it should be noted). But the underlying insight connecting seemingly disparate disciplines was Jung's. So was the idea that symbolism may have a 'psychogenetic basis'. However, Freud had been first on the publishing field. He had marshalled his evidence to show that the syncretism of disciplines and the analysis of their symbolism further corroborated his own analytic theories.

Freud's general technique in these essays was to present detailed accounts of beliefs and practices surrounding taboos and tribal totems that were held by various primitive cultures in Australia, North America, and Africa, and then to explain them through analytic theories of neurosis. He saw both taboos and totemism as symbolic expressions of the prohibition against incest. The totem of the clan was a symbol of its kinship and thus a warning against any intermarrying within the group, so that actual blood-relationship was replaced by totem kinship. Taboos also had their basis in 'the horror of incest' (the title of the first essay). There, the focus of taboo restrictions was directed upon the priest or chief with *mana,* a mysterious power almost like electricity. An underlying emotional ambivalence fueled the taboo, for it derived its internal force from an unacknowledged desire to do what was forbidden. In its punctilious, unquestioned, and ceremonial observance by those who believed in the taboo, it was very similar in nature to the obsessional neurosis which is equally irrational in its manifestation.

By implication, Freud was thus asserting that the 'points of agreement' between 'prehistoric' and 'primitive' man, and man today, are that both have the Oedipal conflict as the determining factor in their development and both are motivated by a libido that is solely sexual. Neither totemism nor taboos 'really' have anything to do with man's ethical development or his religion, although they are surrounded everywhere by religious beliefs and practices.

Jung had written at some length in his letters of late 1909 and 1910 about incest-prohibitions as the psychogenetic basis of much ancient mythology. Certainly Freud's theoretical interest in infantile incest predated that of Jung. But the basic connection between psychoanalysis and 'archaeology' (whether prehistoric or primitive) was made by Jung, and so was the insight that religious practices thus unearthed might be a symbolic form of contemporary neurosis.

The final split between Jung and Freud was marked by their terse exchange of letters in January, 1913. In January and February of 1914, Freud wrote the brief essay, 'On the History of the Psycho-analytic Movement'. It is wounded and defensive, transparently designed to set the parameters of psychoanalysis by recounting its past as a finished fact. Adler and Jung become mere mistakes in Freud's judgment. The function of this essay as a vent for spleen is obvious enough. But there is a point where its revisionism is worth noting, for it relates to the matter of appropriation and pre-emption just discussed.

In his account of the expansion of psychoanalysis to other fields of knowledge from 1908–13, Freud seemed to assume an attitude of becoming modesty, as this author of *Totem and Taboo* wrote:

> this development is still in its infancy; it has been little worked at, consists mostly of tentative beginnings. . . . The workers [in these other fields] can bring only the qualifications of an amateur to bear on the technical problems of these unfamiliar fields of science. These workers, who derive from psycho-analysis, make no secret of their amateurishness.[69]

However, he is clearly sniping at Jung – although Jung's extensive, prolifically detailed *Wandlungen* of 1913 is not even cited among the shorter, less ambitious works by Jones, Rank, and Abraham – for this entire section was intended to show that the 'Zurich school' or the 'Swiss' had been excluded because they were not true analysts. If Freud and his followers were 'amateurs', how much more the one laboring in the field who was not really an analyst!

Freud gathers under his wing all of these 'workers,' next stating that 'most of these applications of analysis naturally go back to a hint in my earliest analytic writings.'[70] That hint proves to be the idea that the study of neurosis should not be limited to psychoanalysis but extended to other fields. The 'workers' of 1908 through 1914 are listed. Not only is the early Jung mentioned vaguely as giving 'mythological material later. . . elaboration',[71] from 1909–10, but *Jung*'s ideas from 1909–10 on 'the correspondence between schizophrenic phantasies and the cosmogonies of primitive times and races' are attributed to one of his *followers* of 1911.[72]

Freud's 'hint' proved to be a 1907 paper that drew parallels between 'the psychology of religion' and 'the ceremonials of neurotics'.[73] Yet that essay was not a seminal one extending analytic theory to other fields of knowledge.[74] Its study of religion could not even be called cursory for it only alluded to the very general religious practices of prayer and penances, and then only to those of Christianity.

What is telling here is the claim itself, as well as the shuffling of dates of precedence so that Jung's actual priority is erased.

This unacknowledged pre-emption has not been limited to Freud. Two of Jung's analytic concepts have proved fundamental to the discipline and passed into the general discourse, usually without any recognition that they derived from the marginalized Jung.

Jung first set forth the theory of complexes in his 1907 essay, 'The Psychology of Dementia Praecox',[75] developed out of his experiments with his Word Association Tests from 1904–07. The tests themselves have become a standard diagnostic tool, and Freud acknowledged in 'On the History of the Psycho-analytic Movement' that 'the concept of the complexes has achieved . . . widespread popularity' among analysts at that time.[76] He complained that it was such a 'convenient' and 'often indispensable term' that analysts tended to use it indiscriminately simply to mean repressed material.[77]

By now, the concept of complexes has passed into such general acceptance that it may be difficult to realize that Jung was its originator. Jung continued throughout his life to develop complex theory, far beyond its 1907 beginnings. It has remained a cornerstone of Jungian analytical psychology, for in Jungian theory a primary function of archetypal symbols is to bring the repressed content of the complex to the attention of consciousness. This Jungian theory of complexes can prove particularly useful for the non-Jungian literary critic, as well as the more general psychologist, so it is well to let Jung define the complex for us.

In 1934, he wrote:

> A 'feeling-toned complex' . . . is the *image* of a certain psychic situation which is strongly accentuated emotionally and is, moreover, incompatible with the habitual attitude of consciousness. . . .Complexes are in fact 'splinter psyches'. The aetiology of their origin is frequently a so-called trauma [or] an emotional shock. . . that splits off a bit of the psyche. Certainly one of the commonest causes is a moral conflict, which ultimately derives from the apparent impossibility of affirming the whole of one's nature . . . Complexes are not entirely morbid by nature but are *characteristic expressions of the psyche* [italics his] . . . The *via regia* to the unconscious is not the dream, as [Freud] thought, but the complex, which is the architect of dreams and of symptoms.[78]

In 1940, he added:

> Now it is an axiom of psychology that when a part of the psyche is split off from consciousness it is only *apparently* inactivated; in actual fact it brings about a possession of the personality, with the result that the individual's aims are falsified in the interests of the split-off part.[79]

Another equally familiar concept that derived from Jung was the idea of extroversion and introversion as the basic orientations of the personality toward the outer world. He proposed this in *Psychological Types,* the first book he wrote after splitting with Freud. It was published in 1921 but conceived during the five years following the break. Jung euphemistically termed these years his 'fallow period',[80] but in reality it was a time in which he approached mental breakdown. He wrote of *Psychological Types* in his autobiography: '[It] sprang originally from my need to define the ways in which my outlook differed from Freud's and Adler's.'[81] Even more than the theory of complexes, the theory of extroversion–introversion has become part of psychology generally – it has become part of popular psychology.

More than specific theoretical concepts has been contributed by Jung to the discipline. Freud had found Jung's idea that mankind may possess some common inherited psychic experience – a 'psychogenetic memory' – to be fruitful indeed. This may be seen in the instance of *Totem and Taboo.* (And consider also the idea advanced in the fourth essay there that an original experience of a 'primal horde' may still be experienced in modern totemism.)

There were also definite Jungian echoes in Freud's essay 'The Uncanny' ('It often happens that neurotic men declare that they feel there is something uncanny about the female genital organs. This [uncanny] place, however, is the entrance to the former [home] of all human beings, to the place where each one of us lived once upon a time and in the beginning'[82]), as well as his later theory of the inevitable psychic fluctuation between the Eros and Thanatos instincts . . . not to mention the entire theory of the Oedipal conflict. All are archetypal in nature.

Later psychoanalysts have also found this idea of a 'psychogenetic memory' fruitful, although its source has gone generally unacknowledged. It is not so much that Jung has directly influenced them as that his entire outlook is congenial with many of the developments of the mainstream theorists, of whom he is not really seen as being one. Andrew Samuels suggests a new category of the 'unknowing Jungians,' and lists contemporary analysts who have what he calls a 'Jungian orientation'. They certainly would not consider themselves Jungians: among them Melanie Klein, the British school of object relations theorists, and particularly D.W. Winnicott, Heinz Kohut, Ernst Kris, Jacques Lacan, Judy Mitchell, and R.D. Laing.[83]

Most of them would loosely be classified as Freudians. Yet they work with the characteristically Jungian ideas that innate psychic-structures profoundly affect the individual's present psychological experience, or that the unconscious may have a non-destructive and creative side, or that incestuous fantasy is symbolic, or that analytic theory should be concerned with the feminine process of maturation rather than only the masculine one, or that schizophrenic experiences may have significant meaning.[84]

But many Jungians have recognized this theoretical sympathy, for one of the most significant schools of contemporary Jungian thought uses the theories and clinical findings of the object relation psychoanalysts Melanie Klein and D.W. Winnicott. Focussing upon the characteristic ways in which the ego develops in the early years of life, these Jungians work with Jung's ideas on the role that archetypal symbols play in the process of individuation as well as Klein and Winnicott's theories about the psyche's innate structure of symbols that determine the pre-Oedipal development of the ego. Belonging to what is termed the Developmental school, these Jungians do not reject the traditional Jungian transpersonal study of myth but rather shift their emphasis to the more clinical side of Jung's thought.

This school of Developmental Jungians could benefit their own field of ego psychology if more widely known. Certainly they could also enrich contemporary literary criticism, so heavily influenced by the tenets of psychoanalysis.

But this centralizing of Jung – that has gone on for half a century – is generally ignored by non-Jungians.

3

Exclusion

Exclusion is the final step in silencing the tabooed voice that has been marginalized. There are two conscious exclusionary defenses that the individual may use against painful materials to block them off from awareness: censorship and suppression. These have been employed by the psychoanalytic movement against dissident theorists such as Adler, Melanie Klein, and Karen Horney, but particularly Jung. Censorship and suppression characterized the reactions of Freud's partisans early in this century, and still do.

Today, poststructuralist literary critics tend to follow the lead of these psychoanalytic patriarchs in excluding Jung from any relevance, as is usually the case. Most such critics see Jung only as the marginalized figure he became for the psychoanalytic mainstream. Jung for them is the Jung identified with the now-outmoded myth criticism of the 1960s and 1970s, and thus somehow associated with their own structuralist past that they would prefer to censor and suppress. But he was more than that to begin with. An examination of the mechanism of this 'official' censorship and suppression may enlighten literary critics, if not the defenders.

The censorship began surreptitiously before Jung had even left the Freudian orbit, with the formation of the 'Committee' in July 1912. The circumstances surrounding the creation of the Committee have already been discussed: the camp was being formed protectively around Freud because Adler had broken away and Jung was also showing definite signs of dissent. Absolute secrecy was pledged by the seven members, and none of the larger psychoanalytic group were to know of it – especially Jung (who was at the time of its formation smarting under Freud's exclusion of him in the 'Kreuzlingen gesture').

Jones first broached the idea to Freud, describing the potential members in a way that was reminiscent of Freud's own metaphor of the censors at the borderline of consciousness who guard against traumatic thoughts: 'a united small body, designed, like the Paladins of Charlemagne, to guard the kingdom and policy of their master'.[1] This censorship was reified with Freud's presentation of the antique classical intaglios to the 'Paladins'. Freud himself had long worn a ring, one with a head of Jupiter. These rings probably designated their wearers as the seven lesser Olympian gods who acknowledged Jupiter as their king. (No goddesses here!)

The Committee carried on a secret correspondence until 1936. Their activities included the control of membership in the International Psychoanalytic Association and the branch societies, the management of the psychoanalytic journals, and translations of Freud's works into English.[2] This Committee thus played a central role in the formation of the discourse. The censorship could extend to those on the Committee itself if they dissented. Such was the case with the member Sandor Ferenczi, who gradually moved away from his original closeness to Freud and Freudian theory.

Ferenczi had long been Freud's warm friend and supportive follower, until the last years of Ferenczi's life in the early 1930s. The partisans have accounted for his deviance by dismissing it as being due to the effects of his last illness. The motivation for dissent, however, is not necessarily relevant to what the dissenter is proposing. What Ferenczi proposed in his final major paper, presented to the Psychoanalytic Congress of 1932, was that one of the cornerstones of Freudian theory might be empirically false.

Familiar to most students of the psychoanalytic movement is the story of Freud's sudden realization in 1897 that what he had taken to be accounts by his patients of actual childhood seductions were instead accounts of their childhood sexual fantasies. This is Freud's famed 'seduction theory'. In turn, this led to his theory of hysteria and contributed to his general theory of sexual development. It was a linchpin of the system.

Through his analytic experience Ferenczi came to believe by 1932 that very often neurosis could be traced to actual childhood sexual abuse, and not merely the infantile sexual fantasies of the patient. His paper presented evidence that sexual assaults on very young children were far more frequent than usually thought, could indeed cause adult distortions of personality, and commonly did.

The senior analysts at the Congress were reluctant to let Ferenczi read his paper, and afterwards Jones wrote Freud a letter of condolence 'over the difficulty that has arisen with your oldest and dearest analytical friend. . . . [Eitingon and Brill opposed its reading; but] I insisted that there would be less scandal if we kept it inside the [Association]'.[3] Freud responded by calling Ferenczi 'a sick child'.[4]

Ferenczi had written the paper in German and hoped to publish an English translation in the *International Journal of Psychoanalysis,* since the majority of analysts then only had access to the literature that was in English. Jones assured him that it had been translated and would appear shortly. Ferenczi was one of the original 'Paladins' and still quite prominent, and Jones could not well refuse to publish it in the organization's journal. The paper was indeed set in type for a particular issue. But then Ferenczi died. Joan Riviére, Jones, Brill, and Freud all decided to withdraw it since, as Jones wrote to Freud, it could 'only discredit psychoanalysis'.[5]

And so this was done. The paper remained in German until Jeffrey Masson translated it into English in 1984.[6] The question of possible veracity did not seem to be raised, although today's discoveries of the widespread incidence of child abuse would seem to support Ferenczi's insights. But the issue here is not that of convenient hindsight, but of the insistence on decorum about a matter which, after all, involved much possible suffering by patients.

This maintenance of decorum could be extended even to Freud himself, although posthumously. Particularly 'sensitive' subjects were quietly muted or erased by partisans.

The early friendship between Fliess and Freud was one such subject. It was generally known to Freud's close circle but not much discussed since it was known to be a painful memory for Freud. This was a touchy area of Freud's history for, as Freud himself wrote Ferenczi, 'Fliess's case' involved for him 'a part of homosexual cathexis'.[7] But this period was an important one, for during these years from 1887 to 1904 Freud developed his basic theory of psychoanalysis.

The letters between Fliess and Freud were published in German in 1950, edited by Anna Freud, Marie Bonaparte, and Ernst Kris. Anna Freud, of course, was his daughter; Princess Bonaparte his devoted pupil and benefactress; and Kris an important theorist and analyst in his own right who was related by marriage both to the Fliess family and the family of the Freud children's pediatrician. All were protective of Freud, especially in his last years of exile just before World War II. In 1954, an English edition of these letters was published. In both editions, 116 of the total 284 letters were omitted. In some of the published letters, passages were deleted with no editorial indication of the omissions.[8]

In 1985 another English edition was published, edited by Jeffrey Masson, that supplied the missing letters and passages as well as new letters from Robert Fliess's personal collection. The rationale for the omissions in the earlier editions that had been given by Anna Freud, Bonaparte, and Kris took on another dimension: 'The selection was made on the principle . . . of omitting or abbreviating everything publication of which would be inconsistent with professional or personal confidence.'[9]

With Masson's new additions, the emotional coloring of the two men's friendship becomes clearer. So does Freud's 1897 cover-up for Fliess's bungling treatment of his patient Emma Eckstein, who nearly died as a result of Fliess's medical malpractice. All references to this case, for which Freud himself bore some responsibility, had been deleted.[10]

Freud's culpability for their final break-up also becomes apparent, for coming to light here are the letters in which Fliess charges Freud with pre-emption and plagiarism.

But beyond this postscript of letters attesting to reasons for the rancorous end of the friendship, there is revealed a pattern of omissions from those letters written after September 1897 that suggests a suppression of all case histories pertaining to the sexual seduction of children. That September was the point at which Freud changed his 'seduction theory,' and the presence of such case histories in the letters implies that at that time Freud still doubted that his new theory was correct. It is true that somewhat later he became convinced of its truth. But still, his later editors deleted his own hesitancies and any evidence that might disprove his theory.

In *The Assault on Truth: Freud's Suppression of the Seduction Theory*, Masson discussed two of the suppressed passages at length.[11] They were taken from letters written three months after Freud had supposedly come to believe that patient accounts of childhood seductions were really only fantasies. The first such passage showed some trepidation about the conclusions he had just reached, and the second related a case of actual childhood abuse by one of his patients that, he felt, was no fantasy. He concluded this last letter with the heartfelt call for a new motto for psychoanalysis: 'What have they done to you, poor child?' This too was omitted by his later editors.[12] There were other attempted erasures. Paul Roazen has criticized the 'selective secrecy' and 'false idealizations of Freud'[13] by those connected with the Freud Archives, particularly Anna Freud who increasingly took on the role of chatelaine as the years went by. Some of his charges are disputable, but some are not. His account of the arduous process by which Jung's letters to Freud came to light for the preparation of *The Freud/Jung Letters* is perhaps debatable, for he implied that Anna Freud deliberately withheld Jung's letters to her father that were in her possession.[14] When the Jung Institute approached the Freud Archives in 1952 requesting access to Jung's correspondence with Freud, Anna Freud replied that she was unable to find it. However, when Jones needed Jung's letters in 1954 for the second volume of Freud's biography that he was preparing, 'they somehow turned up, and even to the Freud Archives it seemed rather awkward timing'.[15] As evidence, Roazen cited an unpublished letter from Kurt Eissler, Director of the Freud Archives, to Anna Freud. But since this letter was not reproduced, we cannot judge for ourselves.

William McGuire, editor of *The Freud/Jung Letters*, made no such accusation in his introduction to the correspondence. He noted only that although the Jung Institute asked to see these letters Eissler replied that they seemed to have been destroyed in the general confusion when Freud was fleeing Vienna in 1938, and so 'the other side of the dialogue was assumed to have been lost'.[16] McGuire then recounted that Anna Freud suddenly recollected in 1954 that 'all the parcels of correspondence' were brought from Vienna and stored in her house and her brother Ernst's house. The two narratives do not necessarily contradict one another. McGuire simply passed over the puzzling lacuna in silence.

Roazen's charge of 'secrecy' in the case of Anna Freud's own analysis is not so disputable, for he experienced the effects of this secrecy himself. It was generally a well-kept secret, though known to a small group of Freud's intimates, that Anna had been analyzed by her father in 1918. The professional and ethical problems associated with the analysis of someone intimately related to the analyst are obvious. They had certainly been obvious to Freud and his adherents when Jung wrote to Freud in 1910 that he had briefly analyzed his wife Emma.[17] Freud wrote at the time to Jung: 'I should have thought it quite impossible to analyze one's own wife . . . In such an analysis it seems just too difficult to observe the technical rule whose importance I have lately begun to suspect: "surmount countertransference".'[18] His followers have often cited this analysis as proof of Jung's lack of professionalism. Yet analysis of one's own daughter (especially given Freud's emphasis on his Oedipal theory of the libido) would seem to be worse than analysis of one's wife.

Roazen first alluded to this analysis by Freud in 1969, and then mentioned it in print at greater length in 1975. However, he wrote (as of 1990): 'There has never been a discussion of this matter in the professional psychoanalytic literature.'[19] Some of Anna Freud's recent biographies do, although in ways that excuse it. So Raymond Dyer wrote in 1983 that 'no other was likely to have the status or seniority required to analyze Freud's offspring'.[20] In her commanding 1989 biography, Elisabeth Young-Bruehl discussed the analysis at some length, but implied generally that it was primarily done so as to fulfill Freud's general requirement that every psychoanalytic practitioner should be personally analyzed and Anna wished to be such a practitioner.[21] It was merely a job-requirement, in other words. The most salient point here is not the deliberate exclusion practiced by the mainstream Movement, but the continuation of these efforts up to the present. This whole artificial control of dissent by the Freud Archives specifically and by psychoanalysis generally, has drawn considerable criticism within the field. Literary critics who keep abreast of psychoanalytic theory may be aware of this current revisionism, but they have not much considered the implications for their own field that has been so influenced by Freudian thought. Feminist psychoanalytic critics certainly have, many returning to the point at which dissenting theorists such as Karen Horney and Melanie Klein were marginalized.

But other critics have not. Psychoanalysis is still the discourse that defines what is said, or that is modified or revised, or that is defied. It is not so much recognized by literary critics that 'psychoanalysis' is not synonymous with depth psychology, for Jung's 'analytical psychology' also belongs to that field. Yet in other regards, literary criticism today is characterized by intense self-consciousness, attending to what has been shut out from attention as well as what has been included.

Jung's marginality and voicelessness should interest the poststructuralist critic. Psychoanalysis has influenced modern criticism profoundly, not only directly with its theories of repression and resistance but also indirectly with its techniques of reading this repression and resistance when it occurs. The critic has learned from the psychoanalyst how to train the eye for the presence of repressed material in the seemingly unrelated behavioral details. This is true even for the feminist critic who, however critical of Freud, still uses his methods to track the systematic repression of the feminine voice and experience. These critics might consider the extent to which the discipline of psychoanalysis itself has parameters drawn with the desire and strong intent to control – to repress, one might say. The very figure of Jung that is familiar from myth criticism is skewed. It is the Freudian version of Jung, which in turn is the Jung of 1912 at the point of his break with Freud.

The general exclusion of Jung from the province of literary criticism took place early, for the complexity of his theoretical system and the great range of his work has been increasingly neglected.

The early critic Maud Bodkin drew upon his ideas about underlying archetypal structures to human experience.[22] More usually, critics of the 1950s and 1960s employed Jung's vast knowledge of unfamiliar mythologies and religions for their own studies of literary works that showed parallels to these mythic patterns. Jung's *Collected Works* were a gigantic treasure-trove of esoteric materials, a source of sources. However, such critics tended to use only a few volumes: *Symbols of Transformation, The Archetypes and the Collective Unconscious,* and sometimes *Psychology and Religion: West and East.* The chapters on the hero archetype in *Symbols of Transformation* and the essays on the Mother and the Rebirth archetypes in *The Archetypes and the Collective Unconscious,* were particular favorites. It was unfortunate that the *General Index to the Collected Works* did not come out until 1979, for it would have eased the job of such critics considerably. Usually ignored was Jung's edifice of theory about the archetypes and their function that he constructed in the decades following his break with Freud. All that critics took from his analytical psychology were his general ideas that there is a collectively shared unconscious and that a transpersonal structure of archetypes informs human experience.

It seemed at first that Northrop Frye's influential criticism of the late 1950s was Jungian, for his *Anatomy of Criticism* proposed that archetypal patterns underlie all literature.[23] But he and his followers were at pains to distinguish his criticism from Jungian theory. To be sure, literature drew upon the timeless archetypal levels of human life and could be 'anatomized' according to which archetype dominated the literary work. But Frye was speaking only of the self-referential world of literature, to be seen in its myths and formal structures. The ageless aspect that was collectively known, the archetypal symbols that related to this collective level and drew their emotional power from it – all of this related only to the universe of literature. The critic need not posit anything more far-reaching than this.

As poststructuralist critics of the 1980s looked back at structuralism to understand where they had come from and what they had left, Jung was dismissed even more summarily. One would think that the debt of structuralism to Jung's earlier ideas would be clear. His priority is obvious from his mature works of the 1930s, 1940s and early 1950s such as *The Structure and Dynamics of the Psyche, The Archetypes and the Collective Unconscious, Aion: Researches into the Phenomenology of the Self,* and *Psychology and Religion: West and East.*[24] In those works he considers ways in which the fundamental 'structure. . . of the psyche' is shared by all mankind, archaic or contemporary, Western or Eastern, and is to be seen in farflung cultural beliefs and practices as well as in individuals' behavior.

Typical assessments of Jung's contributions were made by Frank Lentriccia and Edith Kurzweil. In his overview of current literary criticism, Lentriccia mentioned Jung only as a way of distinguishing what Northrop Frye is not. It was Claude Lévi-Strauss of the late 1950s and 1960s who was the progenitor of structuralism: 'Historians of structuralism . . . assign fundamental significance to his ideas . . . [and] his concern with the global reach of myth.'[25]

Kurzweil too ignored any parallels between Jung and the structuralists, following the lead of the French structuralists whom she was chronicling.[26] The leading French structuralists such as Lévi-Strauss and Lacan reformulated or revised Freudian theory, attempting to break free of the monolithic psychoanalytic establishment that grew up after Freud; but like Freud these structuralists neglected any possible contribution that Jungian theory could make.

Kurzweil defined structuralism in a way that certainly recalled Jung in his letters of 1910–12, as well as his mature theoretical works of the 1930s and 1940s: 'Structuralism [is] the systematic attempt to uncover deep universal mental structures, as these manifest themselves in literature, philosophy and mathematics, and in the unconscious psychological patterns that motivate human behavior.'[27] It was Lévi-Strauss who was the trailblazer with his study of 'the unconscious nature of collective phenomena [that] discover[s] principles of thought that are universally valid.'[28] Since there was no mention of Jung's prior work, her implication was that Lévi-Strauss's 'attempt to systematize myth'[29] was more or less original with him, particularly since Lévi-Strauss was termed the 'father of structuralism' in the chapter heading. And she portrayed the efforts of structuralists in the late 1950s to trace common roots between individuals' dreams and social myths as deriving from *Totem and Taboo* alone.[30]

Yet, as Paul Kugler noted, Lévi-Strauss's reformulation in 1949 of the Freudian unconscious was 'almost identical' to Jung's division of the unconscious into the personal and the collective strata. Further, Lévi-Strauss's concern with universally recurring structures that take protean forms in cultures and social myths was very close to Jung's theory of archetypes, first set forth decades earlier.[31]

Almost worse than the general neglect of Jung by literary critics have been their misunderstandings of him. Very often, these misunderstandings seemed to result from the critics' lack of familiarity with more than a few of Jung's works, or, in some cases, with more than a few of his essays. Here also the same texts were cited again and again in footnotes and bibliographies.

Often, Jung's rather unsophisticated essays on literature have been taken to represent Jungian literary criticism generally, although they are definitely products of their time. That time is not only the 1920s and 1930s when they were written – for they share the heavy-handedness characteristic of psychological criticism then – but, really, European High Romanticism. His essay on the relation of psychology to literature presented a picture of the Poet that is a throwback to a century earlier. This is particularly apparent since he wrote the essay in 1930, far after the advent of modernist art and literature.

The artist is the 'creative personality'[32] who draws upon the collective layer of archetypal symbolism, 'not the only one who is in touch with the night-side of life [for] prophets and seers are nourished by it too'.[33] The most creative artists are those who draw upon mythic materials to which all may respond.[34] The artist may be an individual but is also 'an impersonal creative process', 'a moulder of the unconscious psychic life of mankind'.[35]

The inadequacies of this sort of Romantic criticism may be seen in Jung's essays on Joyce and Picasso. Clearly it is a case of the critic not measuring up to the artist. On Joyce's *Ulysses*: 'The book can just as well be read backwards, for it has no back and no front, no top and no bottom . . . This singular and uncanny characteristic of the Joycean mind shows that his work pertains to the class of cold-blooded animals and specifically to the worm family.'[36] On Picasso: 'I can assure the reader that Picasso's psychic problems, so far as they find expression in his work, are strictly analogous to those of my patients . . . Harlequin gives me the creeps.'[37]

More usually, Jung made the mistake common to the ideological critic who presses literature into the service of something other than itself: whether the literature in question was mediocre or excellent seemed to make no difference so long as it proved his point. One would think from Jung's long, reverential study of Longfellow's *Hiawatha* that as literature it ranks with *King Lear*.[38] Jung terms this 'poetic compilation of Indian myths' as 'an epic' that illustrated the mythic journeys that the archetypal

Hero must make.[39] He finds parallels to this story of Hiawatha in the myths of the Pueblo Indians, Buddhism, Christianity, and the Gilgamesh epic. By implication, the literary merit of Longfellow's poem is of similar ranking. And probably the only literary critics who have heard of Rider Haggard's novel *She* are those who have read Jung's essays on the anima archetype.[40]

Freud's own critical essays on literature show a similar reductiveness, perhaps because they too were written in the early decades of this century. The calibre of the literature makes little difference to him either. This is transparently so in his chapter, written in 1907, on Jensen's short story 'Gradiva'. After an extensive analysis of the main character and the plot of the story, Freud noted that what particularly had interested him was that he found a 'confirmation of my findings [in *The Interpretation of Dreams*, just published] in imaginative writings. I was thus more than a little surprised to find that the author . . . in 1903 [had written about] the very thing that I had believed myself to have freshly discovered.'[41]

His later literary essays all find the same central psychological trauma to be at the core of widely disparate literature: the Oedipal conflict as experienced by the male child. So his analysis of a scene in Shakespeare's play *The Merchant of Venice* (1913) traces its significance back to the archaic mother and the forms she assumes during a man's life.[42]

His famous essay 'The Uncanny' (1919) opens with a long study of Erich Hoffman's story 'The Sandman' and the source of its 'quite unparalleled atmosphere of uncanniness'.[43] This source turns out to be the male child's fear of being castrated by the retaliatory Oedipal father, represented by the Sand-Man. Freud's 1928 critique of *The Brothers Karamazov* uses the novel to shed light upon the neurotic personality of its author who was dominated by dread of a castrating father and his own 'repressed homosexuality'.[44]

These excursions by Freud into literature that primarily served to illustrate his psychoanalytic theory have been leniently regarded by Freudian critics, who have gone far beyond Freud's own tendency to consider the art to reveal the writer's own neurosis. Such critics instead have used Freud's theoretical and clinical findings to construct sophisticated theories of literary criticism. Why cannot Jung be granted the same leeway?

There is an extended essay by Jung that points the way to another kind of psychological criticism. His 'Answer to Job' (1952)[45] could almost be called poststructuralist in its analysis of the Biblical books of *Job* and *Revelation.* Here Jung looks at the character of God in *Job* as one would a character in a story, and considers the split between the way this figure was taken by the Jewish culture at the time of the book's composition and the way it is likely to be taken by the contemporary reader. Yahweh is in definite need of greater individuation for 'his actions are accompanied by an inferior consciousness', as shown by the 'moral defeat he had suffered at Job's hands'.[46]

If 'Answer to Job' in general is rather New Historicist, Chapter 12 in particular is deconstructive. Here Jung analyzes the symbolism, structure, and language of *Revelation* to show the internal inconsistencies of the Biblical book and its gaps between intent and actual execution. Jung looks at the persona of John (not the unknown author himself as so many Biblical scholars have done), and at John's crumbling defenses against projecting his own destructive and negative desires onto the figure of the avenging Christ. The results, Jung says in this unorthodox reading of *Revelation,* are theological contradictions, and an unassimilated use of 'heathenish'[47] allusions and myths in this supposedly Christian account of a Christian apocalypse.

However, the only Jung that many literary critics know is the one to be found in the same few essays: 'On the Relation of Analytical Psychology to Poetry' (1922) and 'Psychology and Literature' (1930).[48]

Thus Robert Mollinger declares in *Literature and Psychology* that 'for Jung art is suprapersonal', with the individuality of the artist taken over by the force of the archetype.[49] The artist is a kind of passive conduit for thoughts and symbols from the collective unconscious.[50]

Although Edith Kurzweil and William Phillips state that they have not excluded 'any legitimate points of view' in their collection of the standard psychoanalytic essay,[51] they include none who are Jungian and merely refer to Jung in their introduction as one of the many who 'tackled the mysteries of creation and the secrets of individual works'.[52] Elizabeth Wright is more briskly dismissive in her survey, *Psychoanalytic Criticism.* In her brief chapter on 'archetypal criticism' (by which she means Jungian criticism), she faults such criticism for not considering the individual writer or the historical culture[53] since Jung and his followers search for '"vulgar" Jungian symbolism'[54] in specific literary works.

For many, Jungian criticism thus is identified either with his own aesthetic notions or with myth criticism. 'Archetypal [Jungian] critics and myth critics are interchangeable terms,' states Shirley Straton in *Literary Theories in Praxis.*[55] Archetypal critics, she continues, use his archetypes of the psyche to interpret a writer's meaning,[56] the archetypes thus evidently being static in their denotations.

Given this general historical assignation of Jung, it is understandable that for many critics Jung's value seems as faded as those simpler bygone critical days. Generally ignored has been Jung's insistence that archetypal symbols are dynamic rather than fixed in their meanings, always having some compensatory function for the individual who experiences them. Their appearance in cultural myths may underline their collective nature and reveal their meaning, but myths are only one vehicle for the protean form of archetypes.

This protean quality distinguishes Jung's concept of archetypes from that of Plato, although often the two are confused and Jung is called Platonic. But Plato's Ideas are different from Jung's archetypes. Platonic archetypes were created by the demiurge, and exist in the world of the ideal. They are transcendent by nature. We only know imperfect copies of them in this mortal world. Jungian archetypes derive from human experiences repeated countless times over eons, and we know their manifestations today in an emotionally direct way because the form they take is in some way compensatory to our conscious lives. They are immanent by nature.

This key distinction between Platonic and Jungian archetypes is central to Jung's whole theory of analytical psychology, and I will return to it in the next chapter. It tends to go unrecognized by literary critics, who dismiss Jung's relevance for them as they dismiss Plato's.

Thus Eric Gould's attempt to account for the persisting relation between myth and literature – a brave attempt, considering that he made it in poststructuralist 1981 – begins by showing Jung's irrelevance to his project because of Jung's 'essentialist' understanding of archetypes.[57] He is a 'fundamentalist'[58] in that his archetypes exist only in a transpersonal realm beyond the individual. He 'seeks meaning . . . in a transformational process beyond language, and therefore beyond anything we can possibly know'.[59] Jung's significance thus acknowledged and dispelled in the first thirty pages, Gould devotes the rest of his book to more reputable figures such as Northrop Frye, Paul Ricoeur, Lévi-Strauss, and so on. His judgment of Jung evidently is based upon a knowledge mainly of Jung's *The Spirit in Man, Art, and Literature,* for most of the citations are to this book alone.

Likewise, Mollinger evaluates the Jungian approach as being less flexible than the Freudian one, because Jungians consider that the symbol is always 'supra-personal' while Freudians relate the symbol to the individual's personal experience of it.[60] For Jung, 'the collective unconscious contains . . . tendencies to gravitate in our ideas toward primitive modes of thought. True symbols are expressions of these intuitive ideas and are not related to the personal unconscious.'[61] This is an inaccurate summary, although it is the popular understanding of the Jungian critic. Mollinger's bibliography cites only the usual four essays by Jung on art and literature, taken from *The Spirit in Man, Art, and Literature.*

Wright too holds that Jungian criticism occupies itself only with universal symbols having no relation to the individual or the individual's cultural setting.[62] These archetypal symbols show themselves in 'bizarre and extravagant fantasies that threaten to dissolve the boundaries between self and world'.[63] This is a real misunderstanding of Jung's theory of the function of archetypal symbols, since this is true only in psychosis. *Freud* may believe that art springs solely from neurosis, but *Jung* does not; indeed, he thinks that archetypal symbols more usually work to bring about greater health for the individual.

Even the generally sympathetic critic Paul Kugler, who contributes the brief essay on 'archetypal (Jungian) criticism' in Norman Holland's *Holland's Guide to Psychoanalytic Psychology and Literature-and-Psychology*, makes this error.[64] The theory and technique of free association that actually originated with Jung is ascribed to Freud, with Jung later 'extending this idea'. Jung's own method of literary criticism is taken to represent Jungian criticism generally. Such criticism is considered to analyze only the underlying archetypal structures of the text[65] – the timeless, transpersonal structure that is essentially Platonic.

The section in Holland's book termed 'modern Jungian criticism,' again written by Kugler, really only covers the school of post-Jungian thought that is the most revisionist: that of James Hillman. Hillman (to be discussed in Chapter 4) is an influential post-Jungian psychoanalyst who primarily studies the nature of archetypal images as experienced phenomenologically. Although his work has obvious value for the study of such images in literature and has attracted the attention of literary critics,[66] it is only one branch of analytical psychology.

However, it is a form of psychoanalytic criticism that is congenial with Holland's own reader-response criticism, as may be seen in Kugler's summary of Hillman's analysis of archetypal images that might be useful for criticism: 'Work with images, whether in therapeutic, cultural, or literary analysis, becomes as much work on the process of seeing it as on the object seen.'[67] Such Jungian criticism thus studies the reader's experience of the images and how the literary text brings forth these responses, rather than any more profound function of the archetypal symbols with which the images are connected.

There is another Jung whose thinking is in line with much poststructuralist work, although he is familiar mostly to Jungians alone. Some have recently drawn attention to this other dimension in *C.G. Jung and the Humanities: Toward a Hermeneutics of Culture,* a collection of essays about possible values that Jung might have for the humanist of the 1990s and beyond. Particularly relevant are the essays in the section 'Postmodernism'. They elaborate on this other Jung who is revealed in his *Collected Works* through asides, sudden digressions that turn into chapters, and open-ended analyses of his patients' dreams. One gets the full flavor of this other presence only by reading and ruminating upon the many books he wrote.

David Miller writes of Jung's two sides, what he calls Personality Number One who speaks in the familiar voice of jargon, high-minded certainty, and vaguely bombastic rhetoric, and Personality Number Two, 'the other Jung'.[68] Jung Number Two is the one who doubts, who stresses the slippage between what the ego (or consciousness) proposes and what the Self (or deeper unified core) experiences. Jung Number Two persistently and often ironically emphasizes the tricky unknowingness of the unconscious. It is the Jung Number One who confidently sets forth the meanings of the archetypal symbols almost as if they were signs.[69]

Kugler also stresses this duality of Jung while discussing different ways of knowing meaning, the 'myth of meaning' that Jung held to be man's central psychic quest. There is the Jung familiar to myth critics and structuralists, who focuses upon the archetype behind the psychic experience and the fixed, ultimately transcendent meaning of it. There is also the other Jung, Miller's Jung Number Two, who finds meaning by 'grounding it in the experience of not knowing,'[70] in the fluidity of immediate complex experience.

As the editors of this fine book suggest, Jung's most characteristic technique of reading the psyche – amplification – is very similar to the way in which the poststructuralist reads a text. Amplification is the process of interpretation through an ever-widening consideration of parallels and correspondences from ancient as well as contemporary cultures, and associations with world-wide myths, religions, arts, and histories. It is like the poststructuralist concern with intertextuality and the ways in which the palimpsests are never truly erased but continue to dimly affect the present text being read.

This very technique of exploration was part of Jung's thorough-going critique of consciousness and its tendency to rationalize and compartmentalize experience. Here Jung is closest to the poststructuralist of today, for Jung constantly seeks out ways in which the unconscious supplements, complements, compensates, and undermines consciousness. He set out to 'deconstruct' consciousness and its claims of autonomous control and sufficiency, much as the poststructuralist did the Western tradition of logocentrism.

Jung did so by considering as possibly valid those psychic phenomena that had long been excluded by that logocentric Western tradition, unlike Freud. Since his exclusion originally occurred because he had strayed beyond the boundaries set by Freud and the Freudians, why should not the literary critic also go far beyond their solar system to explore the paranormal phenomena of inner and outer space?

These are general areas of sympathy between Jung's outlook and that of poststructuralism. There are other more specific ways in which Jung, and the post-Jungian group known as the Developmental school, can speak to contemporary concerns and enter into the current ongoing dialogue.

Part II
Rejoining

Introduction

> To have been at the margins is to have been in contact with danger, to have been at a source of power. There are pollution powers which inhere in the structure of ideas itself and which punish a symbolic breaking of that which should be joined or a joining of that which should be separate. A polluting person is always in the wrong. He has . . . crossed some line which should not have been crossed and this displacement unleashes danger. The power which produces a danger for careless humans is very evidently a power inhering in the structure of ideas, a power by which the structure is expected to protect itself.
>
> Mary Douglas, *Purity and Danger: An Analysis of Concepts of Pollution and Taboo*[1]

Those at the margins are not simply existing in a state of vague powerlessness, cast off and rejected by their society. Marginality can be a source of power. This power is not any revolutionary kind of power – that of outsiders who join forces to smash the hegemony. Rather the power comes from the state of marginality itself, and from the dangers that its formlessness poses for the prevailing social order.[2]

For one thing, marginality vests the tabooed with a power to pollute others who have remained within the structures of society so that they too become marginal. But beyond that, it is dangerous because it puts the tabooed in touch with the places in society where there are contradictions or where order is likely to break down, as well as the threatening regions of resistance that have been pushed back beyond the boundaries which the society has set for itself. The rules by which one avoids pollution make visible the boundaries of the society, as the very presence of taboo signals the dangers to society.

So it is that the anthropologist studies the areas around which there are taboos as a way of gaining insight into the unexpressed values and fears of the society, attempting in this way to understand the group's mores and considering taboos to have the significant social function of helping to preserve order. Thus anomalous creatures are subject to worldwide taboos because they seem to defy formal categories.[3] What is considered dirt, or pollution to be cleansed or avoided, is always relative to the particular society.[4] Mary Douglas terms as 'pollution behavior' those actions by which the group attempts to avoid any contaminating contact with the tabooed.

In this context, Freud's remark to Jung in 1910 is revealing:' 'My dear Jung, promise me never to abandon the sexual theory. . . We must make a dogma of it, an unshakeable bulwark.' In some astonishment [Jung] asked him, 'A bulwark – against what?' To which he replied, 'Against the black tide of mud – ' and here he hesitated for a moment, then added, 'Of occultism.'[5]

One should consider the significance of Wallerstein's 1987 admission that 'the Jungian Movement . . . has endured worldwide as an alternative therapeutic system',[6] while continuing to insist on Jung's marginality to the psychoanalytic Movement. This 'pollution behavior' by Wallerstein vests Jung with some kind of continuing power for the group. Originally it was Jung himself and the dynamics of his relationship with Freud that were taboo. By now, it is not so much his filial betrayal as his ideas themselves that represent the danger. What kind of ideas are these?

From the beginning, Jung showed a willingness to entertain the possible import of psychological experience that is not necessarily empirically measurable, namely paranormal phenomena. He rejected little out-of-hand. When he decided that the field of alchemy might contain answers to questions about the nature of the collective unconscious that he was then pondering, he taught himself medieval Latin so that he could read the untranslated alchemical manuscripts.

These are Jung's ideas that broke the Freudian 'structure' and provoked his continuing rupture with Freud and the Freudians:

> The human psyche has a collective substratum to its unconscious that has evolved through its experience of the world over eons of time, much as the human body has evolved with collectively shared physical characteristics.
> There are essential gender differences that cause different modes of gender development, with neither gender being superior or inferior but rather complementary to the other.
> The collective, timeless patterns of psychic experience are expressed by means of archetypal symbols. These archetypal symbols from our collective unconscious are among the primary determinants of our behavior.

All of these ideas have the underlying assumption that a person's present individual experience can connect back to an archaic collective experience. One could certainly say that they are colored by 'the black tide of mud of occultism' which Freud so feared, if by occultism one means the study of supernatural forces or agencies, those that are outside the natural world. In the last analysis, Jung's theories are 'unscientific' because empirically unprovable.

Of course, the same charge of occultism can be levelled against Freud, with his libido theory, primal scene, Oedipus/ Electra complexes, and Eros/Thanatos instincts. All of these Freudian theories themselves seem archetypal in that they are thought to be collectively experienced with a universal meaning, no matter what the individual's history. More to the point, none are empirically provable and thus, they too are 'unscientific'.

Donald Spence has made this point cogently, arguing that the claim of psychoanalysis being a science is a metaphor only.[7] Setting up the generally accepted criteria for a discipline to be considered a science, he shows that psychoanalysis fulfills none of them: the data to support hypotheses should be in public domain and freely accessible; early theories should be continually revised according to later evidence; and conclusions should be based upon evidence, not authority.[8] He zeroes in upon the Freudian concepts of the primal scene and the Oedipus complex, both key elements in Freud's libido theory, and comments crisply: 'So long as the rules are unknown by which early events are transmuted into later behaviors, we will always be appealing to an empty concept.'[9]

Thus the very thoroughness of the marginalization of Jung, and the continuing 'pollution behavior' of the orthodox group toward him, should alert poststructuralist literary critics to Jung's possible value after all. Indeed Jung has 'crossed some line which should not have been crossed' and 'join[ed] that which should be separate . . . in the structure of ideas'.[10] He has crossed the line between the natural and the supernatural; he has joined the archetypal with the personal. Let the poststructuralist critic boldly follow by entertaining these possibilities. Jung and many post-Jungians have worked with the *dynamic* nature of the archetypes. This is the area of Jungian psychology that could prove most fruitful for the literary critic today. Jungian depth psychology holds that:

> Archetypal symbols have a compensatory function, for the individual who experiences them.
>
> Certain archetypes are associated with the stages of individuation, with different characteristic archetypes aiding the individuation processes of each gender.
>
> There is a structured development of pre-Oedipal fantasies that accompanies and aids the early development of the ego.

These are probably the most unfamiliar elements of Jungian psychology for such critics, used as they are to the static significations of archetypal symbols from earlier criticism.

4

Marginality and Power

Jung went through his own 'creative illness'[1] after his break with Freud, much as Freud had struggled through the aftermath of his break with Fliess several decades earlier. In Jung's case, he passed through a severe psychological crisis for the next five years that only began abating in 1916 and finally ended in 1920. In his autobiography, Jung calls it 'a period of inner uncertainty . . . a state of disorientation'.[2] Others have termed it a time close to breakdown, or at least one dominated by 'psychoticlike (but not psychotic) mental processes'.[3] Peter Homans considers that Jung connected it with his strong narcissism and gradually accepted it;[4] while Francois Roustang sees it as Jung's successful struggle against schizophrenia.[5]

Jung's own account in his autobiography of his 'confrontation with the unconscious'[6] is mainly concerned to give his dreams and fantasies of this period, thus excising from public view much of his actual biography during this painful time. But still enough information is included about his actions in the outer world to give an idea of the inner dangers he faced.

He clung to the visible proof that he had a palpable, functioning existence in the 'real' world. He reminded himself again and again that he had a wife and five children, and patients who depended on him, and these 'proved to [him] again and again that [he] really existed'.[7] He withdrew from his teaching post of eight years at the University of Zurich because he could not bring himself to read any scholarly books relevant to his field, and also because he felt he could not teach from a position of any certainty.[8]

Meanwhile, he continued his medical practice and allowed the unconscious materials to flow without resistance while he continued his attempts to analyze them rationally. They took the form of dreams and 'an incessant stream of fantasies' from 'an alien world. . . as if gigantic blocks of stone were tumbling down on [him]'.[9] He feared 'plummeting down into them' and becoming their 'prey, . . . plung[ing] into dark depths. . . a soft sticky mass'.[10] At the height of 'working on the fantasies,' they seemed to take on a tangible presence, a literal haunting of the house where he and his family were staying in 1916. During one climactic afternoon when the 'atmosphere was thick' with their presence, the doorbell began ringing though no-one was there. As Jung wrote what these 'spirits' seemed to dictate to him, giving their message form as the *Septem Sermones ad Mortuos*,[11] the air cleared.[12]

Jung wrote little during this time, at least in comparison to his later prodigious output. From late 1912 through 1916 he only wrote three substantial essays, drafts for later revised chapters in *Two Essays on Analytical Psychology*: 'New Paths in Psychology' (1912), 'The Structure of the Unconscious' (1916), and 'The Mana-Personality' (1916).[13] They are transitional essays where he tries to pry loose from Freud's orbit by considering Freud's psychology from the vantage-point of his own emerging psychology. 'New Paths in Psychology' could have been written while Jung was trying to gain converts for the new, reviled psychoanalytic movement almost a decade earlier, for these 'new paths' are those that Freud initiated into the forbidden territories of sexuality.

'The Structure of the Unconscious' is more genuinely transitional, with undeniable echoes of his own experience with the unconscious as he describes it in his autobiography. In this 1916 essay, Jung writes that the materials 'that burst out of the collective psyche are confusing and blinding,' and 'an outburst of fantasy'. This 'unconscious intrudes spontaneously, and sometimes irrupts into the conscious mind like a torrent'.[14] One faces 'the danger of being devoured by the monster of the maternal abyss'.[15]

Sometimes 'unconscious thoughts become audible as voices, or are perceived as visions or body-hallucinations'.[16]

Although to a large extent in this essay Freud's own conception of the unconscious is a given, and thus allowed to define the grounds of the argument, Jung here hypothesizes the existence of the 'impersonal unconscious' and suggests its possible nature. He does not use the word 'archetype' yet, but instead the terms 'historical images' and 'primordial images'[17] and 'object-imagos'.[18] One can see him struggling to formulate his ideas without fully having the language to do so.

In many ways, 'The Mana-Personality' is a continuation of 'The Structure of the Unconscious'. The opening pages continue the portrayal of the anima archetype with which the final paragraphs of 'The Structure of the Unconscious' close, further studying the compulsive power (or 'mana') she seems to possess. The rest of 'The Mana-Personality' develops an idea only covered briefly in the other essay, that of the danger of 'godlikeness' for the individual who confronts the 'collective psyche'.[19]

But midway through this analysis of the individual who unfortunately feels possessed by mana are several paragraphs strongly suggesting that Freud was in Jung's mind as he wrote. 'How very much the doctor is still mana is the whole plaint of the analyst!', Jung comments.[20] The followers of such a personality invest him with still more mana since they 'have such an urge to find a tangible hero somewhere, or a superior wise man, a leader and father, some undisputed authority, that they build temples to little tin gods with the greatest promptitude and burn incense upon the altars'.[21] But this turns the man into 'a flat collective character . . . a father-mask. Master and pupil are in the same boat in this respect.'[22] Somewhat later, Jung remarks that such an inflated personality 'is always in possession of the secret name or some esoteric knowledge'.[23]

In another essay in the same volume, he writes again of this same subject and again clearly with Freud in mind: 'one is a mere disciple, but nonetheless a joint guardian of the great treasure which the Master has found. One feels . . . a moral necessity to revile others not of a like mind, to enroll proselytes and to hold tight to the Gentiles.'[24]

Jung here seems to be privately alluding to the themes in *The Freud/Jung Letters* of Jung's so-called father-complex and the founding of the new 'religion' of psychoanalysis, even the formation of the secret Committee around Freud. Significantly, however, these pointed paragraphs are incorporated into Jung's larger project of delineating his own psychological system, for in this short essay he is describing the negative characteristics of two specific archetypes from the 'collective psyche', the anima and the Wise Old Man. These paragraphs also serve as a conscious warning to himself, as the founder of a nascent psychological movement: 'Master and pupil are in the same boat.'

Psychological Types (1921) was the first book to come after Jung had emerged from this period. Here he is genuinely independent of Freud, not reacting by opposing or by denigrating Freudian theory but instead presenting his own different theoretical conclusions. The book does open with a comparison of Freud and Adler, but Jung seems emotionally distanced from each. They are presented as examples of the 'attitudes' of 'extraversion' and 'introversion', a concept that was original with Jung.

Also original was Jung's theory of personality types as determining the way a person functions in relation to the world, either according to the function type of sensation, intuition, thinking, or feeling (by which Jung means evaluative judgment, not emotion).[25] These theories of personality attitudes and types have attracted much attention from non-Jungians.[26] Indeed, Jung's recognition that personalities may be categorized according to their orientations toward the outer and the inner world has passed into general understanding, without many non-Jungians realizing that the extraversion/introversion theory derives from Jung.

Jung's independence from Freud is even more established with *Two Essays on Analytical Psychology*. Part One, giving his general theory of the collective unconscious and the archetypes, opens by sweeping away the two other major systems of the 'new psychology'[27] that were created by Freud and Adler. One sees the psyche as dominated by Eros, and the other by the will to power. Jung concludes with unexpectedly fervent praise for the Freudian outlook when he writes of Freud and then Adler:

> In the first case, the ego is merely a sort of appendage to Eros; in the second, love is just a means to the end, which is ascendancy. Those who have the power of the ego most at heart will revolt against the first conception, but those who care most for love will never be reconciled to the second.[28]

But still, what a demotion! Freud's is simply one of several possible psychologies, and Adler's is another. Freud's psychology is the starting-point for those who come after him, not the definitive one. The parameters that Freud established for psychoanalysis thus are set aside in *Two Essays on Analytical Psychology,* as he becomes more of an historical curiosity than the grand patriarch.

Jung's psychology is the third that is possible. The fundamentals of his analytical psychology are set forth in the rest of this book: the nature of the unconscious as being divided into personal and collective strata; the 'primordial images' of this 'collective psyche' that are to be seen in worldwide religions, ancient myths, and patients' dreams and case-studies; and the process of individuation, or the creation of a unified Self, as the teleological goal of the psyche. He has broken through the psychoanalytic parameters into his own realm. There is a feeling of boldness about this book which comes from accepting as 'a source of power' that which has made him marginal.

The general outlines of his theories of the 'collective psyche' and 'primordial images' are given here, but the examples proving the theory prevail. The theories have developed out of Jung's own analytical practice and experience. This method of presenting his theoretical system proves to be characteristic for Jung. If his psychological theory differs from that of his predecessors, so does his presentation of it. Reading Jung is very different from reading Freud.

Freud usually reasons methodically from his general subject with its subdivisions, to examples drawn from his observations, to the conclusions that may be drawn. Some of Jung's essays that present his theory of the psyche proceed in a linear fashion. But Gaston Bachelard is a better preparation for Jung than Freud. Fittingly, the subtitle to one of Jung's volumes is *Researches into the Phenomenology of the Self.*[29]

Jung wheels from discipline to discipline, defining his theory through examples. Often he mixes in colloquialisms and 'peasant wisdom'. He tends to present his important generalizations in the center of his essays, and to give the crystallizing theoretical statement almost in passing. The reader finds this crucial theoretical sentence or brief paragraph after exploring the theory as it works in human thought and action. And that is surely the point. Jung is not only outlining his theory of the psyche as developed from his medical observations of human behavior. He is also teaching us how to read experience. He wishes his reader to sense how the unconscious works, how one apprehends the archetypes, how one understands the symbolic dimension of behavior. There is not a sense of closure in Jung's writings.

Nor is there any real chronological order to the rest of his *Collected Works,* for each volume is a collection of essays whose composition spans decades. Some are extensive revisions of quite early essays. Thus in one volume there might be essays that span two or even three decades, all centering around one theme. His system underwent continual modification as his readings and analytical practice broadened his theories.

To understand Jungian analytical psychology, one must realize that he has his own meanings for certain key terms, 'Self', 'ego', and 'unconscious'.

Self, in general usage means simply the essential being of a person, the individuality. Its philosophical meaning of the underlying principle of all subjective experience, or the

Soul, is somewhat closer to Jung's meaning. Self for Jung means the totality of the personality, the unity of all elements of the psyche toward which the individual works throughout life. It is a wholeness in which the ego-personality has integrated the contents of the collective unconscious while retaining its own integrity of the self; but the Self remains as potential only.

For Freud, the ego is the part of the psyche that copes with the outside world by mediating between the inner demands of the id and the outer necessities of social experience. Ideally, it balances the instinctual drives of the id, the moral directives of the super-ego, and outer objective reality. The unconscious of the psyche is made up of the repressed traumatic, painful experiences of one's life as well as the repressed contents of the id.

But for Jung, the ego is identified with the rather limited sphere of consciousness, 'the subject of all personal acts of consciousness'.[30] The ego goes on developing throughout life, widening to include more and more unconscious contents. The preservation of this individual ego in the face of the 'collective psyche' can be precarious, however, for confrontal with the archetypal dimension of experience often is overwhelming.[31]

The nature of these archetypes that derive from the collective unconscious is sometimes misunderstood. Jung emphatically denies that they are inborn ideas.[32] They are instead 'inherited thought-patterns',[33] 'typical modes of apprehension . . . uniform and regularly recurring modes of perception',[34] 'specifically human mode[s] of behavior'[35] that when conscious appear as 'ideas and images'.[36] Archetypes not only draw their allusions from the field of mythology, but may appear also in the central ideas of ethics, philosophy, even science as well.[37]

Jung's full theory of the unconscious is sometimes scanted. His concept of the collective unconscious is well-known and indeed sums up his psychology for many, being that substrata to consciousness that goes beyond the personal unconscious to 'a second psychic system of a collective, universal and impersonal nature which is identical in all individuals'.[38] What is less recognized is

Jung's strong emphasis upon the importance of that personal unconscious, which turns out to be the same as Freud's unconscious that consists of forgotten experiences, traumatic events, and repressed emotions.

The personal unconscious reveals itself in the complex, or 'splinter psyche',[39] that is incompatible with the usual attitude of consciousness but shows itself in compulsive behavior. The complex 'constellates' the individual actions and reactions, to use Jung's term, in quite an involuntary way.[40] Unlike Freud, Jung does not consider the unconscious to be only negative in its effects on the ego. Similarly, he differs from Freud in seeing the complex as 'not entirely morbid in nature' but rather the real '*via regia* to the unconscious' for the analyst, altering Freud's famous statement about dreams.[41]

Contents of this personal unconscious – memories and the repressed aspects of the present situation – are woven about an individual's experience of the archetype, helping to give the archetype its powerful effect. But the archetype is more than personal. It is connected with the collective unconscious; it is 'the content of the collective unconscious'.[42] This causes the capability of the archetype to change a person's psyche, for it mediates between the unconscious and consciousness.

Jung writes: 'There are as many archetypes as there are typical experiences in life. Endless repetition has engraved these experiences into our psychic constitution, not in the form of images filled with content, but at first only as *forms without content*[italics his] . . . . When a situation occurs which corresponds to a given archetype, that archetype becomes activated.'[43]

It is not only the individual's experiences that determine the forms in which archetypes appear. As Walter Shelburne points out, different racial and ethnic groups can emphasize different aspects of the collective psyche because of their varying cultural histories, so that one archetype or associated archetypes may be more dominant in a culture than another.[44] The historic experience affecting the group may well summon up specific archetypes for the individuals in it.

Too often literary critics assume that archetypes are self-contained referents with fixed meanings, usually positive in nature though at times negative. Thus the Mother archetype as a nurturing, protective goddess is a familiar figure, as is (though less so) the devouring, chthonic witch. The anima who is sometimes bewitching and doom-compelling, and at other times a soulfully inspiring Muse, is also well-known to such critics. Why archetypes appear one way and not another is seldom considered.

But Jung considers archetypes to be bipolar by their very nature. He does not understand them to be static symbols. *The aspect that archetypes assume for a person is determined by the person's attitude toward the unconscious, positive if it is a responsive attitude or threatening if it is not.* For if archetypes by nature are bipolar, so is their function.

In general, says Jung, 'the unconscious processes stand in a compensatory relation to the unconscious mind . . . "compensatory" and not "contrary" because conscious and unconscious are not necessarily in opposition to one another, but complement one another to form a totality, which is the self.'[45] The archetypes work in a compensatory manner too.

Certainly the permutations they may take are many, as the long volumes in Jung's *Collected Works* attest. But still one sees that they act in polar ways: as a promise of the possibility of wholeness when a person is threatened by dissociation, or a reminder of disturbing materials that have been split off from consciousness. Archetypes thus play a crucial role in widening the ego's perception of the unconscious and in its gaining a fuller knowledge of the Self. 'Individuation' is Jung's term for this process of 'coming to selfhood,'[46] a process that is not egocentric but rather opens one to the world of others and 'gathers the world to oneself'.[47]

This protean quality of archetypes should be remembered, as it accounts for their ability to move the individual at a profound, private core of being. Jung uses the religious term 'numinous' to describe the effect of archetypes, saying that their 'feeling-value' decides the nature of the gestalt in which they figure.[48] They alter the individual in definite ways and according to discernible patterns, and act upon the individual's immediate experience.

There always was a strong analytical side to Jung's psychology. He had just begun his practice when he met Freud, and continued it after he had left the Movement. He wrote in his preface to *Psychological Types* that the book was 'the fruit of nearly twenty years' experience in the domain of practical psychology';[49] and he developed his theories from his observations of patients during his lifelong practice. In his later books his focus turned more to religion and esoteric philosophical traditions; but they only augmented his earlier clinical interest, as his running allusions to patients show. One of his very late books is *The Practice of Psychotherapy* (1954), with chapters on abreaction, dream-analysis, and transference.[50]

As Jung continued his practice, his 'Zurich school'[51] grew in influence and attracted adherents. He tried to avoid founding any school of psychology and encouraged a variety of approaches based on his analytical psychology.[52] This clearly was due to his own experience with the Freudian psychoanalytic Movement. He bitterly warned about the dangers of becoming any 'prophet's disciple' and thus prey to 'mental laziness' and 'infantilism' due to the 'deification of the Master'.[53]

But in spite of all Jung's efforts, there has been a systemization of his psychology by his followers and a gradual emphasis placed upon one dimension of his thought – a most important dimension, but still only one. The majority of Jungians have focused almost exclusively on the mythic, transpersonal aspect of Jung's psychology. As Michael Fordham has pointed out, the C.G. Jung Institute in Zurich (the equivalent of the Freud Archives in London) stresses Jung's late psychology dealing with esoterica such as Gnosticism and alchemy, while ignoring or downplaying his earlier analytical interests.[54]

These Jungians use Jung's technique of amplification to pass quickly from the individual's own situation as expressed in dreams and personal experiences to the paralleling collective, archetypal level. Ancient myths, archaic religious practices and beliefs, primitive literatures, all are drawn upon widely. A kind of orthodoxy has grown up among Jungians that is still active, almost mirroring the Freudian one so righteously deplored by Jungians. Anything savoring at all of Freud – anything too 'empirical' or 'scientific,' or that 'reduces' the psyche to the purely personal level – has been as taboo to the majority of Jungians as Jung has been to the Freudians. Even today, there are many Jungians who resist the entire idea of using Jungian psychological tests such as the Gray-Wheelwrights Test, the Myers-Briggs Type Indicator,or the Singer-Loomis Inventory of Personality, on the grounds that they are too empirically oriented and that test measurement itself is too close to the Freudian idea that psychology should be a 'science'.

This is the version of Jung that is generally familiar, certainly to the myth critics and the structuralists. It dominated the field of analytical psychology for several decades and still does to a large extent.

For most Americans, it sums up the field. Some know of another Jungian school that is allied with this Classical school('Classical' because it adheres to Jung alone), though with different sources and terms.[55] It is termed Archetypal Psychology by its American founder, James Hillman. Hillman's writings began appearing in the 1970s, and his influence has grown since that time among American critics who have found his work with archetypal images to be quite compatible with the analysis of literature. His writing style is certainly closer to the literary artist than the psychologist, and thus is more familiar to these critics and more attractive. Especially congenial to reader-response critics is Hillman's belief that the phenomenological experience of archetypal images is crucial to their meaning.[56]

While Jung is a major influence on Hillman, Hillman thinks he has gone beyond Jung to use materials from all of Western culture,[57] a puzzling deficiency with which to charge Jung. Other influences are Henry Corbin, an Islamic scholar who considers archetypes to be the fundamental structure of the imagination, and Edward Casey, a philosopher who writes of the 'extrapersonal'.[58]

Hillman's main focus is on the immediate experience of archetypal images. Our phenomenological intuition of them, he thinks, leads us to the mythology behind the image. The myth in turn leads us to experience the image more profoundly, so that it moves us at a deeper emotional level.[59] For Hillman, therefore, there is a distinction between the personal aspect of the archetypal image and its universal quality; and for him the preferable emphasis should be upon the mythic and the transpersonal, 'Gods, spirits, ancestors'.[60]

Hillman is mainly interested in studying the ways in which archetypal images assist in the making of the 'soul'. He never exactly defines this term that is crucial to his psychology, save for saying that it is the tertium between matter and mind.[61] It is that which 'grants meaning, enables love, and motivates the religious sense,' Samuels says in his summary of Hillman's psychology.[62] As Hillman accurately comments: 'In its speaking about soul, archetypal psychology maintains an elusive obliqueness.'[63] He tends to define metaphors by using more metaphors, with a full sailed rhetoric indeed.

Archetypal Psychology may be well-received by some American literary critics, but others within the field have been more critical. Samuels notes that among Jungians generally, this school is 'controversial'.[64]

Shelburne considers Hillman's Archetypal Psychology to be an alternative to Jung's analytical psychology rather than a development of it; and he sees 'real incompatibilities' between their two concepts of the archetypes.[65] In his view, Hillman rejects any distinction between the transpersonal archetype and the personal image of it, the form that it takes and the meaning of that particular form for the individual. All psychic experience turns out to be archetypal, no matter how personal its origin might seem to be.[66] The archetypal dimension is inflated at the expense of the actual, limited world of the individual who experiences the image. Everything is 'deliteralized'.[67] This also means that the social and historical contexts of the individual are erased as being unimportant.

Only the Classical school and possibly Hillman's Archetypal School are familiar to American literary critics. However, there is another branch of Jungian analytical psychology that originated in Great Britain in the 1930s and has increasingly influenced American Jungian analysts. This group works with those psychoanalytic theories that are compatible with Jungian thinking, particularly those of the British Freudian Melanie Klein. In many ways this school heals the old Freudian/Jungian rupture, offering real possibilities for new growth. It has much to offer literary criticism, although it is relatively unknown in the United States. Its strong emphasis upon the pre-Oedipal stage of ego development especially is in line with the direction that much feminist criticism has taken.

After World War Two, analytical psychology began evolving into distinct schools although they were not systematically formulated for some time. In 1967 Gerhard Adler noted that the 'orthodox' Jungians adhered to Jung's original ideas, while another group he termed the 'unorthodox Neo-Jungians' also employed the psychoanalytic concepts of the Freudians Erik Erikson and Melanie Klein.[68] He himself was sympathetic to the 'orthodox' group.

Ten years later the eminent 'Neo-Jungian' Michael Fordham also distinguished between these groups, noting that the 'Zurich group' was primarily concerned with the religious and mythological side of Jung's thought while the 'London group' practiced it clinically with the aid also of British psychoanalytic object-relations theory. But he noted that little had been written on these latter developments.[69] Both Adler and Fordham are editors of Jung's *Collected Works*.

The most even-handed overview of these Jungian schools is by Andrew Samuels. He terms the 'orthodox' or 'Zurich' group the Classical school, since they remain close to Jung's texts, and the 'Neo-Jungian' or 'London' group the Developmental school, as they are more generally interested in the development of the individual's ego.

The rise of this London school in the late 1930s coincided with the power-struggle within the Freudian analytical establishment when Freud's family and his Viennese followers emigrated from Nazi Austria to London in 1938. In many ways, the London school of Jungians was directly influenced by this Freudian civil war. Americans are not generally familiar with this situation, yet it bears upon the evolution of Jungian analytical psychology.

It was the same old scenario, but with more determined participants.

The Freud family settled in London after a dramatic rescue from Nazi Austria by Ernest Jones. The Nazis had invaded Austria in March 1938. Freud wanted to stay in Vienna until the end, but Jones was determined to get him and his family out.[70] He arrived in the city to find Freud's house occupied by Nazis, and Freud's daughter Anna taken away to Nazi headquarters (but released a day later). As a prominent British citizen, Jones was able to use his influence to get Freud's family their exit permits from the Nazis, and was also able to persuade England to take in the Freuds during a time when European nations generally were unwilling to take in those fleeing from the Nazis.[71] Freud's Viennese circle had resolved to leave with him if he decided to go, and they did this as best they could about this same time. Finally in June 1938 Freud, his daughter and his wife left Vienna for London.[72]

For its part, the British branch of Freudian psychoanalysis had been taking on its own distinct shape since its formation thirty years earlier as the British Psycho-Analytical Society. Ernest Jones had established it, serving as its president until 1944. It was affiliated with the International Psychoanalytical Association (IPA) founded by Freud, and in the beginning was quite in line with the orthodoxy that Freud demanded. Its membership was deliberately restricted to be sure that the members were 'genuinely interested' in psychoanalysis.[73] By the 1920s many members had been analyzed by Freud in Vienna, and became the center of this evolving British Society.

The ambiance of this Society differed from that of the Viennese Society though. Most of them were not Jewish, but had a strong humanistic or even agnostic bent. They concentrated on theoretical aspects of psychoanalysis that the Viennese Freudians did not, namely the origin of the super-ego (this study would later generate the field of ego psychology) and the psychoanalysis of children.[74] This last particularly proved to be an independent development, although the British analysts believed it to be in line with Freud's own thinking.

The development of child analysis was due in large part to the imposing presence within the British Society of Melanie Klein. Klein is not as well-known in the United States as in Great Britain, where she is still respected as a significant if perhaps unorthodox figure. Originally, she was a second-generation member of the psychoanalytic Movement in Vienna. Though she received her analysis under Sandor Ferenczi and her training under Karl Abraham, she had not been analyzed by Freud himself and thus was not considered to be really part of the inner circle.[75]

Invited by Ernest Jones in 1925 to come to London to lecture on child analysis, Klein decided to stay and in 1926 was elected a member of the British Society. Thus she was a part of it nearly from its beginning in 1919.

Klein introduced the idea that children, even very young children, could be psychoanalyzed, with the analyst interpreting their play as Freud interpreted dreams of free-association in adults. Her extensive work in analyzing young children led her to believe that the super-ego is formed during the pre-Oedipal period, much earlier than Freud had thought. Much of what we know about the pre-Oedipal period derives from Klein's analysis of children. She became increasingly controversial, for she thought that from birth the infant experiences a complex internal fantasy-life that accompanied its experience of its mother.

As she began publishing papers in the mid-thirties that set forth her findings, controversy mounted within the British Society as to whether she was diverging too far from Freudian theory.[76] At the same time, British Jungians who were clinical analysts such as Michael Fordham found her ideas to be more and more compatible with Jungian analytical psychology.

One of the weak points of Jung's psychology was that he had little to say about the psychology of children, and only considered what the child symbolized for the adult. This probably was due to Freud's extensive analysis of the effects of infantile Oedipal behavior on adult behavior, for Jung wished after their split to break away into his own area of psychology. But because of this lacuna, the later British Jungians grew interested in the work of Klein, for Jungian theory seemed to be borne out by her conclusions drawn from working with very young children.

Klein turned to look more closely at that archaic time disregarded by Freud when the nucleus of the ego is being formed, and came to believe that the first three years of life are more important than those of the later Oedipal period for the individual's development. To Klein, the mother is the all-important figure during this time for the child, and the child's relationship to her determines to a large extent the child's later development to the outer world. During these years, the infant and then the young child struggles to come to terms with what seems like ambivalence in the Mother and a matching ambivalence in the child toward her. The seeming ambivalence of the Mother comes from her first nourishing the child, when she seems the Good Mother, and then withholding food and thus life, when she seems the Bad Mother. The child responds to the first with love and the second with hatred, and at first the two Mothers seem split far apart from one another. Gradually the child sees that the Mother is both.

As the two merge into the one figure who seems ambivalent, so the child comes to feel ambivalence too: first love for the Good Mother, then hatred for the Bad Mother, and then guilt and depression for having wanted to destroy this person who is also loved.

The child copes with this experience of outer and inner ambivalence through fantasizing which, in its psychological meaning, is an accompaniment to reality rather than an escape as the word more popularly connotes. Running through the child's thoughts are fantasies first of splitting (the Good Mother is far away from the Bad Mother), then of dissolution (the Bad Mother is annihilated), and then of reparation of the Mother through the return of the child's love for her. These fantasies are not random, but follow a primal pattern that helps the child to deal with outer reality and inner feelings. The whole process is one in which the ego develops in its relation to outer objects, first to the mother, then to objects at a transitional distance from her, and gradually further and further out to the external world.[77] This infantile fantasizing Klein saw as the source of adult symbol-making. Echoes of these primal experiences resonate through those of later adult life as what Klein calls 'memories of feeling'.

Jungians at once saw how close this was to the Jungian theory of archetypes: the splitting of the mother archetype into its polar aspects, the ego's struggle to incorporate its own shadow side, and archetypal fantasies that function to aid this process of individuation. The very idea of a universal archaic process by which the ego accepts ambivalence is archetypal in nature.

By the time that the Freuds and their Viennese followers arrived, there already was some dissension surrounding Klein. The Freuds and the Viennese Society all felt that she had departed too far from classic Freudian theory to be considered 'psychoanalytic', and they disapproved of the whole direction in child analysis that she had taken. Since the emigrés were made immediate members of the British Society and began their practices at once, over a third of the analysts in the British Society by 1938 were continental.[78] Of course, the cachet of their being the originators of psychoanalysis was used in the ensuing battle, especially by Anna Freud, as they tried to 'purify' the British Society and return it to Freudian orthodoxy. The forces supporting Klein came to be known as the Kleinian group. However, the majority of the British Society was in the middle, and uncommitted to either side.[79]

In 1942 the Society decided to bring matters into the open, and began what were known as the 'Controversial Discussions', in which once a month members met to thrash out the theoretical differences between the Viennese and the British analysts. These continued for two years. Well-known in the British Society, these discussions were kept within the fold until they were detailed in Phyllis Grosskurth's comprehensive 1986 biography of Klein.[80] The main issue was whether Klein's work was heretical as was Rank's, Jung's, Adler's, and Reich's, and thus to be excluded as theirs was.

Finally, a compromise of sorts was reached in 1944. The Society's Training Committee decided that the theoretical differences could co-exist within the larger framework of the British Society. (The Training Committee was a crucial one, for it oversaw the training of future analysts who thus were future adherents of the various groups.) In outrage, Anna Freud resigned from the Training Committee, and Edward Glover, who executed Jones's administrative duties as Chair and supported the Vienna faction, resigned from the British Society as well.

In 1946 it was decided that Viennese analysts could train their own students; Klein and the Kleinians, theirs; and the uncommitted middle (now called the 'Independents'), theirs. This compromise, however, made the split in British psychoanalysis permanent without really reaching any solution to the more basic question of orthodoxy – or whether there even should be such a thing in a discipline purporting to be a 'science'. So the situation has continued up to today.[81]

In a retrospective essay, Michael Fordham recalled how Melanie Klein's work seemed to him as a ranking British Jungian analyst in the 1930s. He classified her with Freud and Jung as the great psychological innovators, and termed her theoretical analysis of children 'groundbreaking' and 'breathtaking'.[82] She alone used play by children in analysis as the equivalent of free-association in adults. She found that during in-depth analysis children developed a transference based on unconscious fantasies, that Fordham considered archetypes; and this extended the analytic concept of transference. As Fordham and others recognized at the time, her work could be the basis for their own Jungian study of child development. Indeed, as Fordham saw it, his own work (so very influential among the Developmental Jungians) would not be 'comprehensible' without understanding Klein in addition to Freud and Jung.[83]

Fordham himself was a founding member of the British Society of Analytical Psychology in the early 1940s, and its first Chair. There had been an earlier Analytical Psychology Club that met to discuss Jung's new theories as they issued from Zurich; and then, formed between the two World Wars, the Guild of Pastoral Psychology that was interested in promoting Jung's ideas about religion. But the British Society of Analytical Psychology was the first that could be termed a group of professional Jungian analysts.

The rift that soon developed between the Analytical Club and the Society presaged the larger rift between those Jungians focused exclusively on the mythic, transpersonal aspect of Jung's thought and those also interested in his clinical side. So the Club wanted to keep itself separate from the Society, letting the Society concentrate upon clinical study and the training of Jungian analysts. This bifurcation of Jungian groups has continued in other countries where Jungian analysts began to organize themselves. Fordham hails it, saying that 'the London group takes pride in being the first to initiate this pattern of organization'.[84] However, one could also lament this rending apart of Osiris.

Jung had always disliked the idea of any organized Jungian school of analytical psychology. However, Jungian analysts were finding that some kind of formal organization was necessary in order to train future analysts, and Jung reluctantly went along with the formation of such societies. Although he knew of the British efforts in the late 1930s to form their Society, they expected him to have mixed feelings about it. But they managed to persuade him that such a Society was necessary, and he became its first president in 1944 – protesting though that he would not take an active role, as he did somewhat later when they began a clinic. The British Jungians convinced him to let his name be used so that it would be called the C.G. Jung Clinic, and he eventually agreed.[85] Jung thus tolerated and eventually approved the formation of a British school of analytical psychology, but he was not actively (and oppressively) involved in its internal workings and politics as Freud was with the Viennese school of psychoanalysis.

Members of the British Society saw that there were areas of analytical psychology that needed amplification. One was the detailed dynamics of transference and counter transference. Another was the psychology and therapy of children.[86] Jung was generally unsympathetic to this, writing in 1927: 'The child-psyche is still under the influence of the parent's psyche, especially the mother's, and to such a degree that the psyche of the child must be regarded as a functional appendage of that of the parents. The psychic individuality of the child develops only later.'[87]

While Jung saw little value in child psychotherapy, British Jungians disagreed. To Fordham particularly, the work being done by Klein and the Kleinians seemed to dovetail with Jung's concept of the ego and his theory of archetypes. In the 1930s Fordham began collecting clinical materials from his own practice with children. Again and again, he found evidence that archetypal images dynamically affected the child's experiences during the first two years of life. Where classic Jungian theory held that the individuation of consciousness only begins with adulthood and that the Self only develops in adulthood, Fordham came to think that there is a primary Self that is present from birth. In his own way, Fordham was doing for traditional Jungian analytical psychology what Klein was then doing for traditional Freudian psychoanalysis: pushing the inquiry about ego development back into early childhood years, and using the theories of the master to explore the master's blind spot.

Like Klein, Fordham came to think that the ego is structured by the second year, and that the child's relationship to the outer world is influenced by fantasies during the development of this ego. Its consciousness evolves along with its relationship to the outer world (largely comprised of its mother), following a pattern of deintegration as the ego encounters the world and then reintegration helped by the archetypal images that the child fantasies. These archetypes are embodied for the very young child by its experience of the external world, sometimes fulfilled by it and sometimes clashing with it, but affecting the child's maturation in either case.[88] Fordham was concentrating more on the individual than the mythic or transpersonal aspects of the situation; and here too he differed from the Classical Jungians.[89] British analytical psychology thus provided a middle ground between what seemed to many to be an over-emphasis by Klein on the infant's internal fantasy-life and later theorists such as D. W. Winnicott who primarily considered the child's later relationship with the external world.

In late 1950s, British Jungians who had been working with children began meeting regularly at Fordham's suggestion to discuss materials learned from their practices. In 1960, these analysts formed a Children's Section within the Analytical Society, and began Child Analytical Training. In the mid-1960s, Fordham introduced the idea of clinically observing the infant, not only the child.[90] This was the logical extension of his theories of ego development during the first two years, but it was a radical departure from the classical Jungian analytical practice. As Fordham stated in 1989: 'There has grown up a body of knowledge sufficiently characteristic of the Society's members for a London school of analytical psychology to be defined.'[91]

All of this warrants the attention of the literary critic. A psychoanalytic critic would find clinical material in Jung and the Developmental Jungians that is valuable precisely because it comes at the familiar from the unfamiliar viewpoint. For those critics who are more adept with non-Jungian psychological theory, therefore, it might help to begin by noting parallels between Jung and those whom Samuels calls 'the unknowing Jungians'.[92]

Jung thought that there is an innate impulse toward wholeness and a healing power within the individual to bring this about. He considered there to be a positive aspect to the unconscious that helps consciousness toward wholeness; and this assumption also underlies Winnicott's analytic theory, especially his studies of the important role of play in the development of the ego. Jung first argued in *Symbols of Transformation* that often incestuous fantasy symbolizes a more profound and collective experience than an individual's sexual trauma, developing this insight with increasing sophistication in subsequent books. This too is close to Winnicott's views, nor is it really dissimilar from Jacques Lacan's argument that the patriarchal phallus is symbolic.[93]

Jung and later Jungian analysts have thought that sometimes regression in analysis can be valuable, 'provoking infantile reactions . . . but at the same time activating [archetypes] which have a compensatory and curative meaning'.[94] Ernst Kris also holds that analysis can work with a helpful regression. Jung's theory that there are parts of the psyche split away from consciousness, or complexes, has influenced psychoanalysis generally, and Gestalt therapy, transactional analysis, and Winnicott (with his idea of 'true' and 'false' selves) specifically. The entire emphasis on the pre-Oedipal relationship with the mother by the Developmental Jungians is in line with the object-relations school of psychoanalysis.

This is generally overlooked, although these other analysts interest psychological literary critics considerably. Lacanians too will have little to do with Jung, although Lacan's conception of the collectively experienced 'signification of the phallus' seems curiously archetypal. Admittedly the two psychologists differ greatly in their views on the nature of the unconscious, with Lacan's the familiar Freudian storehouse of repressions: for Lacan, the primal repression begins when the child acquires language and enters the (Oedipal) Symbolic order of the Father, deferring desire for the mother, and the endless deferral of desire inevitably continues into adulthood. Yet somehow this 'Nom du Père' who is associated with language does not seem so far from Jung's archetype of the Masculine that is 'the paternal principle, the Logos, which eternally struggles to extricate itself from the primal warmth and primal darkness of the maternal womb'.[95]

Moving beyond parallels that help to orient the non-Jungian reader, such a critic should plunge into Jung's

Collected Works themselves. An excellent way to understand how archetypes might work in literature is to see Jung's theory in praxis. Good essays for this purpose are those in *The Archetypes and the Collective Unconscious* and *Aion: Researches Into the Phenomenology of the Self* on the specific archetypes, and on a case-study of one patient's individuation-process in *Archetypes.*[96]

His analyses of dream-symbolism that appear in many of his essays are also valuable in this regard, as an insight into the technique of reading such archetypal symbols. As the Freudian method of reading dreams is often employed by the literary critic – attention to condensation, sublimation, the latent content, and so on – so should the Jungian technique of reading dreams be used.

Jung stresses the amplification of dream materials, the elaboration of the dream-image through its parallels in 'human sciences' such as mythology, folklore, religion, and ethnology.[97] The sequence of dreams supply their own context for the individual. The meaning of the dream-symbols is not independent from this context. The dreamer develops his own vocabulary of dream-symbolism. Part of the meaning of these symbols, however, must be their archetypal level since it is this dimension that gives the dream its feeling of urgent significance. The dream itself is compensatory in nature, counterbalancing the dreamer's conscious life in some way.[98]

If archetypes are not static in nature, neither do they appear randomly to an individual. The process of individuation is a progression inwards as one comes to know oneself (or at least most of oneself), with specific archetypes associated with each step. Samuels warns against the over-literal expectation that the archetypes will be encountered in any formulaic order,[99] for individuation itself is rarely a tidy, orderly progression toward wholeness. The salient point for the literary critic is that certain archetypes *are* connected with different stages of the process.

Usually the first experienced is the Shadow, or the symbol of the dark, inferior, repressed side of the conscious personality. This is the most accessible because the closest to the personal unconscious. The admission of this

Shadow-side is necessary before one can proceed further, to the recognition of the anima by the man or the animus by the woman. Since the anima/animus is probably the best-known of the archetypes to the non-Jungian critic, it is enough to say that the anima symbolizes the man's inner feminine nature and the animus the woman's inner masculine nature, projected outward onto one of the opposite sex.

The realization that this archetype is really an inner part of oneself that has been projected outward, and thus that one is really psychologically androgynous, leads to the profounder point where one encounters archetypes of the unified Self. For the woman, this archetype of the Self characteristically is the Chthonic Mother or the Earth Mother; for the man, it is the archetype of the Wise Old Man.[100] Other archetypes of the Self are the Child, the Mandala, and the 'God-image'.[101]

Jung has certain presuppositions that must also be held by the literary critic who would work with his theories and findings. Jung assumes that the personality has a potentially unifiable core of being. Psychic wholeness is a possibility, if seldom achieved, for it is the goal for which a person strives. Fragmentary meaninglessness is not a final reality in itself. Communication, even communion, with others is possible; or else the entire idea of the collectively experienced archetypes would be irrelevant, and the analytic process between doctor and patient quite futile.

Of course, this is also true for all depth psychologists, including and especially Freud (*pace* deconstructive critics). 'Where id was, there let ego be', proclaimed Freud as the desired objective that one struggled toward. Whether this core of unity is called 'Self' or 'ego', still it remains a possibility.

The literary critic who would work with Jungian analytical psychology must also hold basic presuppositions about literature. There *is* an inner core of meaning to literature that the reader can aspire to understand. The reader's response to literature is *not* purely subjective but the result of something objectively present in the literature.

The ground of connection between reader and literature, the cause of their interaction, are the archetypal materials present. As the analyst is pulled into a participating involvement with the patient because of the activating archetypal materials in the patient's dreams and experience,[102] so the reader is engaged in literature because of its archetypal dimension.

Nor is the literary creation fully independent of its creator, a world made by its author that then goes spinning off on its way. It is a 'work' that came from human labor, not a 'text' that has been mysteriously found. The configurations of archetypes in the literary work are due to the author's presence as creator, with the reader responding to the work precisely because of the collective experience that is evoked. To a great extent, its archetypal materials give the literary work its power to create response and understanding in the reader.

Past myth critics usually studied the ways in which characters or authors proceeded on a journey toward wholeness, and the assumption was that the quest was successful thanks to the transpersonal archetypes that helped along the way. But Jung has as much to say, perhaps even more, about the various ways in which individuation fails or at least is highly problematical. The appearance of the negative aspects of the archetypes is one sign that this is happening, and the complex is another. The role of archetypes in complexes, their effects on resistant patients, their dangers for the conscious ego when it identifies with them, all are presented at length by Jung since so many of his essays contain extended illustrations from his analytic practice.[103] Here is where Jung could be taken further by the critic than before.

In addition, the critic should remember Jung's *complete* analysis of the process of individuation. Those hostile to Jungian thought have often portrayed the process as only concentrated upon the individual's subjective inner development, a kind of narcissistic navel-gazing. But Jung himself characterizes the process as one which causes a person to be freed from 'the petty, oversensitive world of the ego' with its 'touchy, egotistical bundle of personal wishes' into a 'widened consciousness' that knows an 'absolute, binding, and indissoluble communion with the world at large'. And sometimes that outer world poses a greater barrier to individuation than the individual's own psyche. There may be 'collective problems requiring collective rather than personal compensation'.[104]

That is, sometimes it is the 'world at large' that requires and calls forth archetypal compensation instead of merely individual problems, if the person is to manage any kind of individuation. Thus archetypal materials may be activated because of the outer collective situation. As Jung says: 'The processes of the collective unconscious are concerned not only with the. . . personal relations of an individual to his family or to a wider social group, but with his relations to society and the human community in general.' The compensatory archetypal materials are all the 'more significant and overwhelming . . . the more general and impersonal the condition that releases the unconscious reaction.'[105]

Thus the method of individuation to be seen in literary works may be due not only to the author's individual psyche but to the surrounding collective situation as well. Feminist critics especially should consider how archetypal materials, such as the figure of the pre-Oedipal mother, may be activated by the outer collective situation in a compensatory way. Jung always asks what the *purpose* of the archetype's appearance might be for a person, and what tendencies in consciousness it compensates. So the literary critic might ask the questions of the literary works that Jung asks as he seeks to understand the psyche before him.

What archetypal images keep re-appearing, clustering into a nexus in the overall perspective of the author's corpus? Which archetypes appear, and with which stages of individuation are they associated? Is there a progression to be seen, or does the author seem stuck at some level? For example, are the archetypes to be seen primarily those of the anima or animus? Or are the archetypes variations of the Self? What seems to be the reason for their appearance, and how does this appearance change the work?

Do these archetypal images show the positive or the negative aspect of the archetype? Are they healing? Do they serve as reminders of unity and wholeness in the midst of dissociation? Or does their presence in the literary work act as Jung says such a presence does in a complex, 'constellating' around the point of repression and forcefully reminding the author and reader of what is split off from consciousness?

The positive function of the archetypes that brings order to chaos may be more familiar to us from traditional criticism. But the negative function that brings the split-off parts of the psyche to the attention of consciousness might interest today's critic more, for these insistent archetypal reminders signal contradiction, rupture, breakdown . . . a literary complex, one might say.

However, whether the archetypes work in positive or negative ways in the literary work, they must in some way be pointing toward wholeness, even if it is never realized in the work. The archetypes present suggest the way. 'The psyche is a self-regulating system', says Jung;[106] or as William Willeford puts it, 'the self knows what is good for itself.'[107] The literary critic needs to consider *how* the archetypes in the literary work help toward wholeness, however broken that wholeness now seems.

5

Jung for Feminists

The excluded Other remains so because of the possibility of contagion, for the curious thing about marginalization is that usually one such group will avoid others that have also been stigmatized. It is as if the one group fears that they will be judged to deserve their exclusion after all: they will be doubly polluted. Yet there can be great power released if these groups join, sharing their various experiences gained as a result of being considered taboo.

Jung and the feminists are a good case in point. Indeed, the pernicious results of Jung's exclusion from the psychoanalytic mainstream are best illustrated by this case. Where Jung anticipated them, feminists have disdained him; where Jung could supplement them, feminists have neglected him. Where Jung and the later Jungians could enlighten them, feminists have remained ignorant.

Women 'have been at the margins' by very virtue of being feminine. Jung's real value for poststructuralist critics is not so much for those who wish to extend psychological theory in the name of pluralism as for feminist critics. He could be most instructive for them, both for his own experience of being made taboo and for what he has to say. Much of his material on the Mother and the Kore archetypes, and his different analyses in case-studies of the feminine process of individuation, anticipate by several decades the work of contemporary feminists interested in gender difference.

However they evidently are not aware of this or wish to deny it, for they do not cite him at all. This is true too for the later Developmental Jungians, who also could contribute greatly to the ongoing feminist dialogue that is concerned with the nature of the ego's pre-Oedipal experience and the possible meanings of the figure of the pre-Oedipal mother. But Jung has been associated for feminists with the old patriarchal 'structure of ideas', either because of his early connection with Freudian psychoanalysis or because his belief in archetypal gender differences has made him seem essentialist. For feminists, Jungian analytical psychology tends to be taboo.

Women have been silenced generally for much the same reason that Jung was by the psychoanalytic movement: their otherness, their own alien reality, their difference from the patriarchal model of self that has already been defined for them. Jung's own intellectual interests were not solely concerned with outer objective reality, the empirically provable, the purely rational, the 'scientific', all those hallmarks of the logocentric tradition. He also studied experience that was irrational, intuitive, and subjective. It was part of reality as he perceived it, even though it was different from Freud's prescribed model of psychic reality. His difference proved to be his own 'source of power', for it led to his theories of the archetypes and the collective unconscious.

Feminists too have turned to examine the patriarchal 'structure of ideas' and especially the 'power by which the structure is expected to protect itself'.[1] During the last few decades, they have gone further, asking: how might this marginalization itself be a 'source of power'? What exactly is the feminine, that has caused us to be marginalized? The earlier feminist emphasis on gender equality has shifted to an exploration of gender difference – more specifically, to an exploration of the qualities of the one gender traditionally defined by its departure from the norm of the other gender. Is there an intrinsic feminine psychology? If so, might there be a feminine kind of writing, and a feminine kind of criticism? Not a psychology of the feminine psychology, literature, and criticism that is characterized by what it lacks of masculine psychology and the masculine traditions of literature and literary criticism, but one that has its own essential nature?

For some time, feminists have severely criticized Freud for describing the man's psychological development and proclaiming it to be the universal experience. As Jung's psychological theory developed from the 1920s onward, he redressed that omission – he re-dressed Freud – for he held that the woman's way to individuation is not the man's way. He has much to say about that different route.

Jung thinks that there are archetypes of the Feminine and the Masculine, that he terms 'Eros' and 'Logos'. The feminine Eros-principle is characterized by the quality of relatedness, the psychic joining and emotional connection with others. The masculine Logos-principle is associated with objective judgment and analytical thinking. 'Women's consciousness is characterized more by the connective quality of Eros than by the discrimination and cognition associated with Logos. In man, Eros, the function of relatedness, is usually less developed than Logos. In women, on the other hand, Eros is an expression of their true nature.'[2] Elsewhere, Jung writes of the male animus that he is 'a creative and procreative being, not in the sense of masculine creativity, but in the sense that he brings forth something we might call the *logos spermatokos,* the spermatic word'.[3]

For Jung, the archetypal principles of the Feminine and the Masculine are *not* the same as behavioral roles that should be followed. Eros or Logos is where we start from. They determine what our quests for individuation will be like. The process of individuation differs for men and women.

For the man, it is 'the battle for deliverance from the Mother', as Jung calls it in his extensive analysis of this struggle in *Symbols of Transformation.* The hero breaks free of the Mother and his incestuous desire for her, reborn as his own autonomous person. Ideally, he eventually accepts the Feminine, but without fear this time as he strives first to separate and then to connect again.

For the woman, it is more an unfolding than a conflict: first an acceptance of her Eros-side, her own sharing in the maternal experience ('maternal' in the emotional, not the biological, sense). Then she gradually differentiates and develops her own autonomous will and Logos. She works first to relate and connect with others, and then to assert her intellectual uniqueness.

Jung's materials on the Feminine have not been acknowledged much in feminist criticism. A number of feminist critics in the 1970s weighed his possible usefulness for feminism but decided that it was limited, all citing one another as they reached this consensus. The unanimity of their judgements has led others to accept their conclusion that there is 'male bias' in Jung's definition of the Feminine.[4]

His description of the Eros/Logos principles is quoted again and again by these critics to illustrate his 'blatant sexism'.[5] It is considered to show that Jung thinks that women are not expected to develop Logos 'since they are thought of as handicapped by nature in all Logos areas'.[6] What is needed is a 'post-Jungian' approach that 'allows women to value their images (archetypally) more'.[7]

This criticism itself unintentionally reveals an androcentric bias, a devaluing of those qualities that Jung associates with the archetype of the Feminine. Why should not men feel equally slighted since they are thought of as handicapped by nature in all Eros areas? The existence of the American Men's Movement suggests that many might. It should be remembered that Jung considers these archetypes of gender to be neutral and unranked principles. In fact, he warns strongly against the identification with archetypes on the part of the individual since this can cause the conscious ego to be 'swamped' by the contents of the collective unconscious.[8]

Another feminist criticism of Jung is that he shows an inordinate interest in male psychology. These critics are generally unanimous here also in citing as proof his emphasis throughout his *Collected Works* on the archetype of the anima, man's experience of his own feminine nature projected outward upon women.[9] Jung says that the Greek meaning of the word 'anima', or soul, defines the nature of this archetype.[10] To these critics, it seems that Jung must be 'denying women soul' since he has already defined the anima as a man's projection of his own nature rather than the objective reality of the woman.[11]

These critics' version of Jungian psychology is so far from what Jung actually wrote about women and men that one wonders why so many Jungian analysts have been women. Clues appear in the feminist criticism itself. The word 'soul' prevails, as does a concern with archetypal 'images' of women.[12] Gelpi thinks that while Jung is too concerned with the male psyche, James Hillman can 'right the balance',[13] a belief echoed by Lauter and Rupprecht.[14] Jung is infrequently cited, if at all, while Hillman's name often appears as a source. Lauter and Rupprecht *equate* Jungian analytical psychology and Hillman's archetypal psychology.[15]

Significantly, these criticisms of Jung are exactly the same as those made by Hillman in his article on the anima published several years earlier than them. There, he sees Jung's concept of the anima as a result of his historical patriarchal culture, only being 'the syndrome of inferior feminine traits in the personal sphere'.[16] He criticizes Jung for 'confusing' the anima with feeling and for calling feeling (or relatedness) a feminine prerogative.[17] Jung is considered sexist for assigning the soul to the anima, since women need to develop it too. Furthermore, Hillman thinks that the woman's equivalent archetype of the animus is limited in that as Logos it only pertains to abstract wisdom and knowledge.[18] So it would seem that these feminist critics are really judging Jung as Hillman sees him.

But in all of Jung's *Collected Works,* he persistently reminds his readers of the many ways in which the Feminine principle has been devalued in Western culture, with pathological results. In *Psychology and Religion: West and East,* for example, he makes a highly novel interpretation of the 1950 proclamation by the Catholic Church of the dogma of Mary's Assumption: in so doing, the Church included the Feminine principle into the male Trinity, and finally achieved the quaternity of wholeness missing before.[19] It is true that he writes more about the anima than the animus. However, one could argue that instead of privileging the man's psyche Jung is pointing out the man's great need for the woman's point of view, as well as the man's deficiency in repressing his own feminine side by projecting it onto the anima.

A more general reason for the dismissal of Jung by feminist critics is their perception of his psychology as essentialist. It is understandable why he would seem like one who 'assumes the existence of an essence of gender . . . unique and absolute', innate from birth.[20] Jung's belief that there are archetypal gender differences has seemed to feminists like a reversion to the traditional gender stereotypes, a psychological justification for the traditional social inequalities.[21] Jung seems like another Old World Romantic who believes in the Eternal Feminine.

But when Jung wrote about the Eros-principle and the Logos-principle, he did not have in mind Eros, the son of Aphrodite, and Logos, the classical Greek quality of reason. He was alluding to the Greek and Judeo-Christian cosmogonies that explained how the universe was created out of Chaos or the Void, in order to define the very different ways in which the genders' perceptions 'create' their worlds.

According to Hesiod, Gaea the Earth-Mother first emerged from Chaos and following her came Eros, who after coupling with her created the universe by associating and joining those elements that belonged together. Creation thus came through connection. According to *Genesis* and *The Gospel According to John*, the Spirit of God (or the Word, or Logos) moved upon the dark formless void, and then created light and then the increasingly subtle divisions of the universe. Creation thus came through differentiation. One cannot say that either account is *better*, only *different*. And this is precisely Jung's point about the archetypes of gender: neither is superior or inferior. They are simply different.

For some time, 'essentialist' has been more or less delivered and received as an insult by feminists, taken as an accusation that one is still caught in the traditional concepts of gender. Their desire to overcome social inequities stemming from gender differences has led them in the past to stress gender equality, and to feel strongly that any return to the familiar stereotypes about essential gender characteristics would only be followed by the old phallocentrism. There was the further implication that 'essentialist' really meant 'reactionary', and that one therefore sanctioned the social injustices that resulted from the traditional concepts of gender differences.[22]

However, this logical leap is not necessarily valid. It could just as easily be argued from the essentialist position that if one half of the human race perceives and values things differently from the other half because of their nature, then any degradation of them by that other half is especially unjust. Any resulting social disparity is especially evil.

Furthermore, Jung is not really an essentialist. The only true essentialist position is the religious one of the fundamentalist who believes that the Deity created the genders simultaneously or synchronously and thus fixed their characteristic differences literally from the beginning of time. To be sure, Jung holds that transpersonal archetypal symbols derive from primeval times, and are an inherited part of our psychic structure. So this is also true of the archetypes of the Feminine and Masculine. But one should consider the *origins* of archetypes: how they are formed.

Jung says that archetypes are the 'accumulated experiences since primeval times[23]. . .deposits of the constantly repeated experiences of mankind. . . recurrent impressions made by subjective reactions[24]. . .the deposit of mankind's whole ancestral experience'.[25] The archetypal image itself is not inherited as part of man's psychic structure, but rather archetypal forms and themes. 'Archetypes are not determined as regards their content, but only as regards their form and then only to a very limited degree. . . The archetype itself is empty and purely formal. . . a possibility of representation which is given *a priori.* The representations themselves are not inherited, only the forms, and in that respect they correspond in every way to the instincts, which are also determined in form only[26]. . . The archetype is a pattern of behavior that . . . possesses a powerful dynamism by means of which it can profoundly influence human behavior.'[27]

So the meanings of archetypal symbols are built up through endlessly repeated historical human experiences that assume patterns over time. As Samuels says of archetypes: 'The content is variable, subject to environmental and historical changes.'[28] Shelburne too notes that different racial, ethnic and geographic groups may quite well experience archetypes in 'distinct cultural forms'.[29] He considers archetypes in general, to form through 'evolutionary processes' as does man's physical organism.[30]

The archetypes of the Feminine and Masculine thus are not pre-determined essences of gender, but the distillation of experiences over time. They are transpersonal because transcultural. Human history has produced these archetypes. The archetypes themselves help to form and shape subsequent experiences. They reproduce these experiences.

How does this differ from the thinking of those feminists who argue that gender differences are caused by our long-repeated experiences with cultural traditions, gender differences being thus 'socially and psychologically created'?[31] Nancy Chodorow may deprecate 'the essentialist view of difference of gender'[32] and criticize as essentialist the psychoanalytic interest in female psychology, particularly by the object relations theorists.[33] But her own argument in *The Reproduction of Mothering* sounds similar to that of Jung.

Here she maintains that the desire to mother is not an innate characteristic of the female gender but rather is the result of women being the primary ones to carry out mothering, 'as they have in most cultures and throughout history'.[34] This is an 'almost transhistorical fact'.[35] This 'reproduction of mothering' by women has come about through 'social, structurally induced psychological processes,' for 'all sex-gender systems have been male-dominated'.[36] In other words, these definitions of gender differences have been held in all societies and time-periods: they have been collectively experienced, and they are transpersonal. That is why they still seem true today.

It is by now a hoary observation that Freud ignored the Feminine in general as he constructed an androcentric model of psychic reality. He characterized feminine psychology as motivated by lack and absence, and it is probably overkill at this point to take him to task for this again. Freud may have neglected the Feminine, but other dissident analysts besides Jung took up the question. Theorists such as Karen Horney and Melanie Klein, once close to Freud but later ejected from the Freudian orbit as rudely as was Jung, focussed on the pre-Oedipal period when the mother is paramount. The later object-relations school of psychoanalysis grew from their findings. So did the Developmental Jungians.

Horney and Klein in particular looked at the figure of the pre-Oedipal mother, generally left out of Freud's system altogether. The early analyst Horney countered Freud's theory that women's psychology was shaped by 'penis envy' by proposing that this theory itself was a defense against Freud's characteristically male 'womb envy', or envy of the women's ability to bear children. This masculine envy in turn stems from the great power of the mother during the first three years before the father takes the center of the stage as Oedipal protagonist.

This 'womb envy' implies, of course, that the definitively feminine organ is considered the truly preferable one to have by both genders. The Phallus may signify cultural power, but the Womb signifies life.

Klein has already been discussed in Chapter 4, as one of the earliest theorists of the object-relations school of psychoanalysis. In general, object-relations theorists are most interested in the early period of childhood when the ego's development is shaped by its relation to the outer world and, most importantly, to its mother. There has been an increasing feminist attention to this pre-Oedipal stage of ego development that is so dominated by the mother. Part of this is due to the wish to turn away from the patriarchal Oedipal concerns of Freudian psychoanalysis, but a more significant reason may be curiosity about the primal time when only the Feminine was known.

In *The Reproduction of Mothering* Chodorow bases her theories about the formation of gender differences upon the tenets of this psychoanalytic school, and in so doing she has coalesced these materials with those from her own field of sociology in a way that at present is widely influencing feminist studies. She holds that the ego developments of girls and boys during the first three years differ, because each necessarily reacts differently to the pre-Oedipal mother according to gender. Little girls define themselves by relating to her and connecting with her sexual sameness to them. Little boys must define themselves in opposition to her, struggling for their separation and autonomy from her.

Thus far, the account of the primacy of the influence of the pre-Oedipal mother upon her child is a familiar one. The nucleus of the ego is formed through its interactions and relations with that first external object, the mother. But then Chodorow makes the unfamiliar, bold deduction that gender differences develop as a result of these gendered reactions to the pre-Oedipal mother.

Girls mature possessing the basis for empathy, the feeling of others' needs and emotions as their own, as part of their 'primary definition of self' while boys do not.[37] Because of the girls' pre-Oedipal connection with their mothers as the same sex, they feel more connected and continuous with others and have 'more flexible or permeable ego boundaries'. Boys, on the other hand, emerge from the pre-Oedipal period with a sense of masculinity that is defined by denial of the mother and the feminine that she represents to them, a 'denial of relation and connection'. Masculinity is distinguished by autonomy and an aggressive independence from others.[38]

Chodorow draws some sweeping conclusions from this. For one thing, the masculine sense of self is more problematic and threatened than is the feminine sense of self, which is more 'stable'.[39] The 'reproduction of mothering' also has led to the traditional allocation of women to the domestic sphere and men to the work-sphere of the external world, with the resulting social power for men. In other words, it leads to male-dominant societies with their associated social inequities. The only solution to these untoward consequences is for men and women to share primary parenting equally, in a 'fundamental reorganizing of parenting'.[40] Other conclusions have been drawn from

Chodorow's basic insights about how gender differences may be created. To be sure, the feminine and masculine senses of self may well be formed in relation to the pre-Oedipal mother. But this need not have the oppressive, negative results that Chodorow anticipates, either in society or in the self. Chodorow sees this feminine sense of self as leading to a need for connection that is too easily exploited so that the woman's own needs are ignored and she is relegated to a position of less social power.[41] Others, however, see this feminine difference as a source of strength for the woman.

Carol Gilligan also considers the feminine sense of self to be determined by the archaic relationship with the pre-Oedipal mother. Because the little girl is the same gender as her mother, she feels no need to preserve her own identity through separation and autonomy as does the little boy. Rather she seeks connection with the mother for she strives to be like her; and later she comes especially to value connection with others through relationship. This in turn leads to a different adult value-system from that of the male, a value-system that Gilligan calls 'the ethic of care'.[42]

This feminine ethic differs from that of the characteristically masculine ethic of justice, for it is a morality built around responsibility for others and care for them. Obviously, this 'ethic of care' can lead a woman to be used unfairly, and to seem to fulfill the old cultural stereotype of the feminine as that which selflessly nurtures and sacrifices at the expense of the woman's own well-being. (Equally, of course, the 'ethic of justice' can lead a man to be cold, inhumanly rational, and ultimately quite solitary in his hubris.) But Gilligan persuasively argues that this feminine concern for relationships and caring for others is a 'human strength,' not any weakness.[43]

Similarly, the feminine characteristic of empathy, or 'intuition,' is considered a source of adult strength by Mary Belenky, Blythe Clinchy, Nancy Goldberger, and Jill Tarule, authors of the award-winning *Women's Ways of Knowing*.[44] In their study, they find that women develop their own self-definition through a circling process away from the external judgments of the world and into a subjective kind of knowing.[45] This subjectivist position pluralistically respects others' experientially gained truths and leads to a 'connected knowing', which emphasizes a 'joining of minds' rather than autonomous, independent thought.[46] This feminine 'way of knowing' grows out of women's valuing of relationships and their openness to new experiences.[47]

This all sounds familiar to anyone conversant with Jung's thought, for it is quite in line with his analysis of the archetypes of the Feminine and the Masculine. 'Women's consciousness is characterized more by the connective quality of Eros than by the discrimination and cognition associated with Logos. In men, Eros, the function of relatedness, is usually less developed than Logos,' said Jung.[48] Is there really any dissimilarity between Jung's statement and these by Chodorow, Gilligan, and Belenky, Clinchy, Goldberger and Tarule?

'The basic feminine sense of self is connected to the world, the basic masculine sense of self is separate.'[49]

'Women not only define themselves in a context of human relationship but also judge themselves in terms of their ability to care. . . The capacity for autonomous thinking, clear decision-making, and responsible action are associated with masculinity.'[50]

'We posit two contrasting epistemological orientations: a separate epistemology, based upon impersonal procedures for establishing truth, and a connected epistemology, in which truth emerges through care. . . The two modes may be gender-related: it is possible that more women than men tip toward connected knowing and more men than women toward separate knowing.'[51]

Chodorow herself proceeds to the conclusion that gender differences are caused by culture alone and therefore can be changed by culture too. 'Mothering' need no longer be an aspect of what is taken to be the Feminine. But still her answer to the question of the causation of gender can only derive from belief, not empirical proof.

To be sure, these authors would resist any comparison to the supposedly essentialist Jung. This, together with his marginal status in the field of psychology, is probably why all neglect to cite his precedence to them or even to mention his remarkably similar theories at all.

Developmental Jungians also have closely studied the effects of the pre-Oedipal mother upon the developing ego of the young child; and their work makes Jung even more relevant to that of feminists interested in pre-Oedipal gender development. For the last sixty years, these Jungians have evolved a Jungian-oriented object-relations psychology, deriving their theories from clinical experience. Michael Fordham in particular studies early childhood and the influence of the pre-Oedipal mother upon it.[52]

Nor is it only a British school any more. In his overview of 'post-Jungians,' Andrew Samuels divides prominent Jungians according to the school they follow: Developmental, Classical, or Archetypal. He lists forty who are Developmental in orientation (more than he lists for the other two schools together), and many are American.[53] One such of especial interest is William Willeford, a practicing Jungian analyst who was a professor of English literature for a long time. His writing is engaging and non-clinically literate, as one would expect of someone who began as a literary critic; and his work is accessible to the reader who is not a specialist in analytic theory. In his latest book, for example, he draws upon literature, religion, his experiences as an analyst, jazz, anthropology, and other sources to make his theoretical points about the 'mother–child dyad'.[54]

The *Journal of Analytical Psychology* should also be a consulted source. Founded in 1965 by Michael Fordham (its first editor), this journal has a decidedly analytical slant but includes articles that could be termed Classical. It is an interesting mix, although it may feel unfamiliar to readers accustomed to a more specialized grouping of articles. Articles on witchcraft and the Penelope episode in Joyce's *Ulysses* jostle studies of female sexuality and of the dreams of anorexic and bulemic women.[55] The journal's book-reviews also are wide-ranging. There is an eclecticism about it that is in itself Jungian.

But the American feminists ignore the work of this entire school of Jungian psychology, as they do Jung. This seems like a blinkered view of the field, given the other congruous points between Jung and feminism. For otherwise, feminists have shown a strong interest in the implications of materials from object-relations theory for feminism, and have given a renewed attention to these earlier female analytic theorists.[56]

This refusal to acknowledge any precedence by such a well-known figure in the field may well be connected to the distinct uneasiness that many feminists feel as they pursue the subject of gender difference. This train of thought seems to lead to the possibility of gender essence.

Chodorow and Gilligan themselves have faced the charge of essentialism from feminists who believe gender is solely a social construct. It might seem that Chodorow is arguing that gender is socially constructed, by countless cultures through time that have assigned certain parenting characteristics and functions to women. Her solution to the problem of social inequities resulting from mothering is to call for both genders to share equally in the parenting process, with all of the accompanying social changes that would be necessary to accomplish this. Yet still she is charged by Toril Moi with having 'a deep-seated cultural (as opposed to biological) essentialism [that] reintroduces age-old patriarchal beliefs in a specific female nature.'[57]

And indeed, Chodorow, in an essay meant to dispose of the idea that there is an 'essence of gender',[58] lets slip a sentence that assumes an inborn maleness that senses gender difference in the pre-Oedipal mother: 'Underlying, or built into, core male identity is an early, nonverbal, unconscious, almost somatic sense of primary oneness with the mother, *an underlying sense of femaleness* that continually challenges and underlies *the sense of maleness*' (italics added).[59]

Chodorow has had a wide-spread influence on academic feminists and literary critics, but Gilligan hit a responsive chord as well among the more general reading public. Typical of the popular reception received by her book, *In A*

Different Voice, is the review that appeared in the American *Vogue* a few months after its publication. This place of publication for one of the earliest of its reviews is itself revealing, being aimed at the generally knowledgeable (and presumably fashionable) reader, but certainly not the academic specialist. The highlight of the article was an interview with Gilligan, and its general angle was that she was the herald of a new way that women might see themselves.

Thus, the reviewer opened by recording her own reaction to Gilligan's assessment of reasons for gender difference: 'To me, it has the charge of a revelation . . . . It is impossible to consider Carol Gilligan's ideas without having your estimation of women rise . . . She reframes qualities considered as women's weaknesses and shows them to be women's strengths.'[60] At the same time, the reviewer dutifully notes that she is 'suspicious' of any supposed gender characteristics as such, 'flattering' or not. Gilligan rejoins that Chodorow offers the most likely explanation for women's 'different voice', namely that women are historically the primary caretakers, but then the reviewer and the author go on without bringing up the indelicate question of gender essence again.

However, others certainly did. The feminist journal *Signs* first reviewed Gilligan's book almost as favorably as did *Vogue,* calling its publication 'an important event' that will 'change the face . . . of feminist thought'.[61] The reviewer saw it as another weapon against the hegemony, 'a critique of instrumental rationality in capitalist, male-dominated society'.[62]

Several years later though, as Gilligan's ideas were digested by feminists, *Signs* took a different tack. Her concept of an 'ethic of care' may have been absorbed into the general public's revised – and more positive – understanding of gender differences by then, as in fact it had. But she was definitely under attack for her 'essentialism', by both psychologists and academic feminists. In 1986 *Signs* sponsored a Forum at which she answered key criticisms, publishing the results.[63] The views expressed typified the opposition.

The four participants seeking to dismiss her conclusions charged that her research was too limited and her evidence insufficient to warrant such sweeping conclusions. Two noted that she did not include enough studies on men.[64] The other two agreed that her book rested on small-scale studies,[65] and complained that women readers have too often accepted Gilligan's conclusions because of their own subjective sense that she is right rather than considering the evidence more objectively. Gilligan had 'oversimplified the case and overinterpreted the data'.[66]

Gilligan countered that her critics concentrated on studies of gender difference that undercut her findings, but ignored the fact that the tests themselves had the built-in bias of using the standards of one gender to judge both. That is, the definitions of 'self' and 'morality' were assumed, but they were the traditional, male-dominated definitions (the very point of her book). She also took the criticism that her women readers have too quickly agreed with her because her ideas 'feel right' as further corroboration of her conclusions.[67] Finally, Gilligan noted that the studies cited by her critics to disprove her points have all-male samples.

But these critics made another, more telling accusation that was not so much scientific as it was ideological: her ideas will simply lead back to the old cultural stereotypes of gender. She assumes that 'gendered behavior is biologically determined'.[68] Her ideas seem tinged with the nineteenth-century ideas of men and women occupying different spheres, and with the historical oppression of women.[69] They support 'gender stereotypes'.[70]

In other words, it is not a matter of whether her findings might be true but whether one should think this way in the first place. This is the real heart of the criticism against Gilligan and other so-called 'essentialists': their ideas might lead to the traditional gender stereotypes, and one *ought not* to think this.

However, as pointed out earlier, it is a fallacious leap of logic to say that such 'stereotyping' must lead to cultural oppression. It could just as easily lead to cultural respect of innate differences. And if 'gendered behavior' is not in any way 'biologically determined', then what of the role of the sexual hormones in human behavior, hormones that are specific to gender? What of women's biological experiences that are specific to their gender: menstruation, child-bearing, menopause? To deny that biology can affect human behavior according to gender not only flies in the face of all scientific evidence, but, at a profound level, perpetuates the old Western philosophical dualism of mind and matter – a denial that is logocentric to the core.

And here one comes back to Jung's ideas of what women and men are like. Gender is not merely a social construct. Whether it has been created during the pre-Oedipal stage of ego development, or whether it is formed by the different phases of biological experiences that each gender knows, or whether it is an essential part of one's being because of mankind's past collective experiences of women and men – still, gender is archetypal difference.

It must be admitted that there is some truth in the feminist criticism that Jung writes less about the nature of 'women's consciousness' as such, than about that of men, although he has much material to offer on the woman's unconscious and the ways in which certain archetypes from it affect her consciousness. But if one is honest, one writes from what one knows for oneself; one writes from one's own consciousness. Jung was male, and at times he wrote frankly from that subjective vantage-point. (Here, in his somewhat wry awareness of his subjectivity, he was at his most non-Freudian.)

What male psychologist today would dare to write this about the female gender as Jung did?

> *Emptiness* is a great feminine secret. It is something absolutely alien to men; the chasm, the unplumbed depths, the yin. The pitifulness of this vacuous nonentity goes to his heart (I speak here as a man), and one is tempted to say that this constitutes the whole 'mystery' of woman. [Compare this with Freud's puzzled, 'What do women want?'] Such a female is fate itself. A man may say what he likes about it; be for or against it, or both at once; in the end he falls, absurdly happy, into this

pit, or, if he doesn't, he has bungled his only chance of making a man of himself.[71]

Yet the bias of the observer here is part of the insight; this is how the woman's 'flexible and permeable ego boundaries'[72] seem to a man's consciousness.

Later female Jungians have written more extensively about 'women's consciousness'. Jung has not written much about the animus archetype, which helps to widen the woman's consciousness so as to incorporate her own Logos side. Jung's concept of the animus seems almost like a logically necessary counterpart to the anima, rather like Freud's notion of the Electra complex that is the equivalent of the man's Oedipus complex.

However Emma Jung, his wife, did explore the nature of this archetype in depth and, as one might expect, her account of it has more of the ring of experience about it.[73] Written in 1934 and then revised in 1955, her book jibes with the tenor of contemporary feminism today in unexpected ways that certainly were unintended by her. Telling in itself is her emphasis upon the negative ways in which this archetype affects a woman, rather than its positive possibilities. Emma Jung purports to describe the woman who is 'animus-possessed' and thus has set aside her own feminine nature.[74] What she really is portraying is the woman who has internalized the beliefs of her male-dominated society, and who thus has internalized its devaluation of the feminine too.

Esther Harding considers the feminine stages of individuation more thoroughly than either of the Jungs.[75] Originally written in 1933 and updated in 1970, her book bears the imprint of that pre-feminist era since it assumes that the process necessitates the presence of a man in a woman's life for her complete individuation. Yet this in itself should not rule out Harding for today's feminist readers, for this is the real-life condition of many women. Those feminists who are impatient with such thinking should remember that it is particularly the situation of those women of color who wish to remain part of their traditional cultures. Harding is especially insightful into what it means for the woman to be the recipient of the man's projections: how it feels to seem his anima, how this changes her own behavior, and above all what this might reveal about her own psychology.

Ann Ulanov's 1971 Jungian study of the nature of feminine consciousness would be the most valuable for non-Jungians interested in gender difference. She reminds us that for Jung individuation, whether masculine or feminine, must involve 'a full awareness of contrasexuality'.[76] That is, the genders are distinguished by determining the contrasting or opposing qualities of each. The feminine and masculine principles are polarities of the 'objective psyche', complementary 'styles of being human'.[77] The polarities of gender are built into the structure of the psyche. Individuation in general is a continuous process of coming to terms with the strangeness of one's inner opposites. The construction of self comes through such reconciliations. Without the gender differences *as psychological principles* a person could not work toward a complete identity at all.[78]

Men and women adopt their gendered 'styles of being human' to varying extents. Like Jung, Ulanov is speaking here of the archetypal Feminine and Masculine principles, not specific behavioral roles to be followed. Since historically the Masculine principle has been of primary interest to Western cultures, the nature of the Feminine principle must likewise be known if one is to understand fully the 'objective psyche'.

Ulanov believes that feminine consciousness characteristically assumes the archetypal attitude that is associated with the Great Mother. Jung has described the qualities of the Mother archetype as 'maternal solicitude and sympathy . . . all that cherishes and sustains, that fosters growth and fertility. . . anything secret, hidden and dark. . . These are three essential characteristics of the mother: her cherishing and nourishing goodness, her orgiastic emotionality, and her Stygian depths.'[79] Typically, Ulanov, says, the woman's understanding of an idea is a ripening process, not a willed judgment. She takes the idea into her consciousness and lets her perceptions grow around it as it gestates.

The woman's experience during menstruation, pregnancy, and birth is of being taken over by outer forces beyond her control; and she responds by waiting and remaining receptive to the natural process that is happening. Similarly, the characteristic feminine attitude is one of openness and receptivity. 'The ego never withdraws or abstracts . . . but rather allows itself to be drawn to the contents [of the idea] and then circles around them.'[80] Her conscious sense of time is cyclical too, waxing and waning in her feelings of energy and creativity as her hormonal changes during ovulation and menstruation affect her perceptions. Her consciousness is characterized by the expectation of change and flux, not finality and closure.

In the most profound sense, then, the feminine ego consciousness is an expression of the woman's bodily experiences that are known by her, day in and day out, month after month. As Ulanov points out, this feminine quality of openness and receptive responsiveness is also 'essential in religious experience'.[81] One thinks of Mary who after the birth of Jesus and the visitation by shepherds and angels 'kept all these things, and pondered them in her heart'(Luke 2:19).

Ulanov's analysis of feminine ego consciousness is close to that of French feminists such as Luce Irigiray, Julia Kristeva, and Hélène Cixous who were exploring the nature of feminine 'difference' at about the same time. But it is highly unlikely that there was any reciprocal influence between them. The intellectual climate of France at that time was dominated by Freudian psychoanalysis, in particular by Jacques Lacan. Ulanov's book was published in 1971, and works by Irigiray, Kristeva, and Cixous did not appear until the mid-1970s; but it is clear that the French writers had not read the discredited Jung or any of his followers. Nor is it likely that Ulanov had read Irigiray, Kristeva, or Cixous. Although the French feminists' work on gender difference was flourishing during the 1970s, it was untranslated until the 1980s and generally unknown by American feminists until then, even those interested in the same subject.

During the 1970s the intellectual climate of France was dominated by Freudian psychoanalysis, and in particular by Lacan's version of it. This was the defined ground of psychological discourse, whether to follow or to oppose. Lacan called for a 'return to Freud' by psychoanalysis, a closer hewing to Freud's earlier theories of the unconscious and to the text of his *Standard Edition* rather than to later interpretations of it. The heretic Jung certainly had no place in Lacan's schema, nor would he for Irigiray, Kristeva, Cixous, or any other French intellectual working within that cultural context. In addition, given the staunch opposition to psychoanalysis by the French Catholic Church that considered it immoral, Jung's decidedly sympathetic attitude toward religion also put him beyond the pale. Finally, his own Teutonic background would have made him suspect. But he could have been consulted profitably by those French feminists who came to question, even oppose, Lacan.

Unlike the British Society that embraced psychoanalysis from its beginnings in the first decade of the twentieth century, the French at first distrusted it because of its Germanic beginnings.[82] This German xenophobia had its historical precedents to be sure, although in the case of psychoanalysis it seems ironic considering its exclusively Jewish origins. But in France of the 1920s and 1930s, psychoanalysis was primarily championed by the artists, to the detriment of its reputation among the medical specialists.[83]

However, this changed after World War Two, possibly because of the dispersion of the Viennese Freudians who in their flight from the Nazis were clearly not to be considered Germanic in their sympathies. Psychoanalysis came to be associated in France with radical politics. Somehow it grew linked with Marxism in its study of how denied contents may still affect consciousness, with the analyst/Marxist attending to what has been repressed by consciousness/the dominant social ideology.

The Parisian 'May-June Revolution' of 1968 cemented this association. During the 'Revolution' university students began an uprising against all forms of traditional ideology, whether expressed by government, employers, or the traditional Opposition of the Left and the trade unions.[84] It was brief, but gripping, as universities, schools, factories, and hospitals went on strike across Paris. It only lasted weeks, and then power returned to where it had always been. But it gave momentum to the growing French 'infatuation'[85] with psychoanalysis. Psychoanalysis had come to be seen as a theoretical ally of the Left.[86]

The 'French Freud'[87] of the time was Lacan, and his brand was set everywhere on psychoanalysis. By the early 1970s Lacanian psychoanalysis had entered the popular culture, with his name a kind of synonym for a nationalist development of psychoanalysis away from its 'Germanic' roots. There was a general fascination with Lacan on the part of the French public as well as the academic intellectuals.[88]

Lacan joined the Paris Psychoanalytic Society soon after his own analysis in 1934, and from the beginning was unorthodox both in his hostility to any institutionalizing within the psychoanalytic Movement and in his theories of the necessarily fragmented nature of the conscious ego. 'Where id was, there let ego be', Freud had said; but for Lacan, the unconscious is a constantly disintegrative force upon the ego, and the reality to which this ego must adjust is necessarily one of social inequities and thus further fragmenting.

Like Freud, Lacan focuses upon the child's Oedipal conflict as central to its development; but unlike Freud, Lacan sees the child's desire for the mother to be really the desire to complete what she seems to lack: the father's phallus. This phallus for Lacan is symbolic not literal in its meaning, for it is the phallus as symbol of social power that is desired, both by the child and, the child feels, by its mother. This completion of, and fusion with, the mother is what the infant at first desires hopelessly; and next it desires identification with this paternal phallus, or signifier of power. The original desire for fusion with the mother thus is repressed and endlessly deferred (though still affecting the conscious ego in unconscious ways) as the child enters 'the world of the phallus', with all of the social privileging on the phallus.

So actually the mother does desire to possess a phallus, for she desires the social power that it confers and she lacks. For this reason Lacan uses the word 'lack' (*manqué*) again and again to characterize women, but he is not speaking as Freud would, of any 'penis-envy' but rather of the woman's wish for the power that the phallus symbolizes in her society, that is full of inequities based upon gender.

For many French feminists, Lacan seemed to make psychoanalysis congenial to women as Freud never did. Lacan, they felt, was analyzing the social reality in which they lived and the effects of patriarchy upon the psychology of women. But others saw Lacan rather differently. Even if we consider the phallus as a social symbol and signifier, it still has a privileged place in Lacan's psychology. The woman is condemned to an inevitable 'lack' because she is not a man, whether socially imposed or not. Luce Irigiray was one of the earliest and most famous critics of Lacan as a phallocrat.[89] Others, most notably Jane Gallop in *The Daughter's Seduction: Feminism and Psychoanalysis*, saw him as sidestepping female sexuality because he subordinates it: woman is lack. Not Other, but lack.

Irigiray was one of several French feminists during the 1970s who raised the question of whether there might be inherent differences between men and women that were due to more than the social 'privileging of the phallus'.[90] Might these differences be reflected in women's writing, or what these feminists called *l'écriture féminine*? Lacan held that the child's desire to enter the father's world of the phallus occurred at the time that it also entered the language system and took on the whole system of signifying symbols that that involved, with the society's structures embedded in its language. So it was natural for these feminist critics to analyze written language for what it revealed about possible gender differences. Might there be a characteristically feminine kind of writing generally, and a feminine kind of literature specifically? A characteristically feminine kind of literary criticism to be practiced?

Hélène Cixous in particular brought this possibility of *l'écriture féminine* into the central focus of French feminist debate of the 1970s. Like other French feminists then, she mounted a critique of the whole patriarchal logocentric tradition ('phallologocentrism,' in the barbarism of the time) that privileges abstract theory and reason. In this masculine tradition, the feminine and all that it 'lacks' is different and therefore subsidiary.[91] Like others then, Cixous considered this logocentrism to be expressed in a typically masculine writing that is didactic, planned, logically constructed, and expositional.

Cixous argues for the female's otherness, not merely her difference, since 'difference' implies a norm against which the different may be measured. This otherness, this '"Dark Continent" is neither dark nor unexplorable.'[92] The feminine nature is open, non-linear, flexible, and fluid in its boundaries, for it is based upon her bodily experience of existence. Not for her any dualism, whether Platonic or Cartesian. The very concept of dualism, with its denigration of the material body, is masculine. Similarly, feminine writing is non-linear, fragmented, 'attempting to "speak the body"'.[93]

These French feminists were generally ignored by American feminists until the early 1980s, for there were few translations available until then. Those who were aware of them were wary, if not hostile. The French critics interested in *l'écriture feminin* seemed unorthodox, even subversive, in their exploration of gender differences, for they were writing at a time when gender equality was stressed. It seemed then that any discussion of gender differences must lead to the traditional social inequities associated with such differences. *Féminin(e)* can translate either to 'female', implying the biological gender, or to 'feminine', meaning the social construct of gender. This ambiguity implied that gender is both biological and social, and seemed to suggest that these French feminists were returning to an essentialism that was inadmissible.

Many American feminists found the entire announced project of 'writing from the body' disturbing. It was attacked as 'incoherent' and 'theoretically fuzzy'.[94] Even those who approved of the general liberating strategies used by these French critics were disturbed by their emphasis upon the physicality of *l'écriture féminine,* and particularly by Cixous' insistence that the female body affects women's writing to such a profound degree.[95] This 'writing from the body' above all seemed to evoke the old cultural and religious stigma of inferiority inflicted upon women.

The possibility of gender essence was troubling for more than political reasons, although such considerations were often there: the study of *l'écriture féminine* was termed 'fatal to constructive political action'.[96] But some also wondered if this study might lead to a 'metaphysics of presence',[97] or be 'ontotheological'.[98] If so, it ran counter to the whole Derridean tendency of poststructuralist criticism and thus was doubly inadmissible.

But by the mid 1980s, these French feminists were definitely modish and taken as the cutting edge of feminism, in more ways than one. By the end of the 1980s there were two distinct factions among American feminists, each claiming to be 'the new feminism': the Anglo-Americans and those interested in the French.[99] The Anglo-Americans accused the French of being 'essentialist'[100] by 'reinforcing . . . patriarchal stereotypes of the Feminine' and neglecting the oppressive social conditions that women face.[101]

Curiously however, the 'French feminists' throughout the 1980s were taken to be only Irigiray, Kristeva, and Cixous. There were other French feminists, many with a decidedly Marxist cast of thought. But, as Jane Gallop has pointed out, it was the American feminists who made the triumvirate solely representative of French feminism.[102] Cixous in particular seemed to captivate Americans with her audacity and wit; and the 'central text' (as Gallop puts it) of this movement made in America was Cixous' essay, 'The Laugh of the Medusa'.[103]

And even Cixous is known to Americans only for her theoretical texts that she wrote in the 1970s. She is better-known in France for her avant-garde fictions and plays. She has moved from her theoretical work in the 1970s to creative works that deal with moments of historical crisis and what they reveal of underlying ethical and historical structures.[104] She has moved closer to what her critics wanted of her, in other words: more involvement in immediate historical circumstances. But she is primarily known by Americans for her theories of *l'écriture féminine.*

By the mid 1980s, this 'French feminism' was the 'most prestigious'[105] of the feminist critical theories on the scene. The phrases 'representations of the body in the text' and 'writing from the body' had become part of the feminist critical vocabulary, functioning almost as shibboleths. Many saw her as more subversive to the patriarchal tradition than any frontal feminist attack. Cixous does not use the intellectual weapons of reason and theory, or any appeal to the facts of the historical exclusion of women or the logical necessity of their inclusion. Her weapons are rather play, laughter, extravagance, and an insistence that any discussion of feminine difference must be expressed in terms of her bodily experience of sexuality, childbirth, mothering.

Her very form of writing seemed a political strategy to undermine logocentrism.[106] Her continual playing is an emancipatory technique[107] – her puns, juxtaposition of learned allusion and colloquial slang, and humor. ('Men say that there are two unrepresentable things: death and the feminine sex. . . Look at the trembling Perseuses moving backward toward us, clad in apotropes! What lovely backs!')[108] This playing is also a characteristically feminine quality in that it shows the 'flexible and permeable ego boundaries' of which Chodorow speaks, rather than the masculine desire for closure.

As these French critics were translated in the mid-1980s, American feminists began to appreciate them for more than their undermining effect upon logocentrism. This French criticism drew upon feminine experience in the most immediate, direct way; and this in itself raised provocative questions for feminist criticism. How might gender difference affect literature written by women? – or literary criticism written by women?[109]

As it has turned out, the general direction of much American feminist criticism has been toward a study of gender difference as reflected in forms of writing that are non-traditional because they are personal writings. So there are more and more critical analyses of women's letters, diaries, and journals. Some feminist criticism is deliberately subjective at times, rather than uniformly trying to preserve the illusion of objectivity.[110]

Beyond this, the study of gender difference by these French critics fits in with a more general poststructuralist interest in 'repressed Otherness',[111] the entire process by which the dominant culture marginalizes certain groups and then declares them invisible.

These French critics perform another service as well. They analyze the source of woman's marginalization, which proves to be her very nature or 'difference'. Their celebration of this difference thus makes it clear how this marginalization might be a 'source of power', in Douglas's sense. The very form of this criticism – its 'strategy of play'[112] – becomes a way of using this power. 'You have only to look at the Medusa straight on to see her', writes Cixous. 'And she's not deadly. She's beautiful and she's laughing.'[113]

Jungian analytical psychology can contribute to this ongoing feminist dialogue. Those who have found 'French feminism' intriguing would do well to consider Jung's comprehensive study of the Mother archetype, the yin principle associated with matter, fertility, and nurturing animal nature. They should consider too Ulanov's analysis of feminine ego consciousness as being fundamentally influenced by the woman's bodily experiences. For it is striking that the French studies of *l'écriture féminine* do not seem immediate and historic (the critics of their politics are right to this extent), but instead primal and timeless. Their characteristic quality is archetypal.

Even their writing style is reminiscent of Jung's when he is writing about the archetypes. His style too mixes together abstruse learning with high-flown emotion-laden metaphors, personal statements, occasional colloquialisms, and Swiss-peasant sayings, as he circles around his central topic to give the sense of how the unconscious works through amplification. Likewise, these French critics who are celebrating feminine difference, juxtapose learning and slang, sometimes in the same sentence. Their style, thus, is without a sense of 'respectable' boundaries, being open, fluid, and lushly poetic in its metaphors.

American feminist critics also have grown interested in the figure of the mother; and here too it is not so much the actual, personal mother who is considered as it is the more general subject of the projection of pre-Oedipal experience upon the mother, and the ways that this symbolic figure shapes our later adult lives.[114] The implications of this for the literary critic are particularly rich, for a whole new dimension to literature opens up. The 'memories in feeling' of which Klein speaks in her essays on this stage reverberate through art as well, and as readers we must look for other aspects of the text than we are used to.[115]

Julia Kristeva had proposed that there is a pre-Oedipal level of experience that she calls 'semiotic' in which the infant feels fusion with its mother, and that this level can be summoned up in avant-garde literature.[116] She does not say that there is any structure to these 'semiotic' pulsations in language, but only breaks in syntax, prosody, puns, and dislocations of expected meanings. Gallop pressed forward on this point to consider the general sort of language that must be associated with the pre-Oedipal level and what significance this might have for the literary critic, since it would be prior to any logical Oedipal narrative. She answers that this level must be expressed in dreams and wish-fulfillments.[117] Meredith Skura suggests another kind of pre-Oedipal expression in literature when she comments at length about archaic fantasies in the literary text. She too fails to offer any possible structure to these fantasies, calling their role 'varied and unpredictable'.[118]

But what if these fantasies are quite predictable? What if there is indeed a pattern to them during pre-Oedipal development that is duplicated in literature?

Klein and then the Developmental Jungians suggest that there is. American literary critics have not paid much attention to these theorists, usually concentrating instead upon those stressing the child's later relationship with the outer world such as Winnicott, Kohut, and Kris. None of these latter theorists work very intensively with the child's inner symbolic fantasy-life. But perhaps the rich body of materials by Klein and the Jungians on this earliest experience of symbol-making could prove very meaningful for literary studies.[119]

Fordham considered that these archetypal fantasies that accompanied the continual experience of disintegration and reintegration included those of the unified Self, growing more and more complex during individuation but not really different in kind. The psychoanalytic literary critic might examine the archetypal fantasies running through a work, consider the influence of disintegration or reintegration upon the work. Such a critic would want to take into account the archaic stage with which those fantasies are associated in determining the overall meaning of the work.

Fordam's suggestion that there is a systematic pattern to these archetypal fantasies has important ramifications for the literary critic, for those archaic but collectively experienced fantasies must then be present for the critic to perceive in literature as well as life.

6

Jung for the Future

Thus Jung should be admitted into the ongoing dialogues of psychological and feminist criticisms, as one whose work proceeds along congruent lines. However, his case is significant for other reasons too, because it raises the larger question about the relation that the marginalized voice should have to the dominant discourse that created the definitions of 'central' and 'marginal' in the first place. This has also been a crucial question for those interested in more general issues of cultural studies, although here the question is usually phrased in terms of race, ethnicity or gender. Should the marginalized follow a separatist route? Or should they push to be included in the larger dialogue, reintegrated into a discourse that is thus reformed and re-formed?

The separatist route has been the more traditional one to take. It has been the one familiar to the extreme nationalist groups. In his classic study of colonialism, *The Colonizer and the Colonized,* Albert Memmi described well the typical first stage of liberation by the colonized. By definition the colonized are the marginalized; so he has dedicated his American translation of the book to 'the American Negro, also colonized'. In this stage, all the previous marks of the inferior status are now taken as signs of superiority over the colonizer: 'He has been haughtily shown that he could never assimilate with others. Very well, then! He is, he shall be, that man.'[1] The marginalized status is definitely preferred.

Memmi wrote his book in 1957, and it predicted the sweeping nationalist movements to follow. As he noted in his 1965 Preface to the American edition, he wrote it originally for the obviously colonized peoples of North Africa, but soon found that it influenced others more subtly colonized in other parts of the world, with colonial police confiscating it from the cells of nationalist militants.[2] And he concludes in his incisive passionate portrayal of the colonial situation that revolt seems the only possibility for the colonized since assimilation is impossible and undesirable in any case.[3] Assimilation or revolt – those were the only possibilities seen then and for some decades to come.

More recently the Palestinian Edward W. Said has written of the honoring of the general state of marginality: 'Marginality . . . [is] not, in my opinion, to be gloried in, [but] to be brought to an end so that more, and not fewer, people can enjoy the benefits of what has for centuries been denied the victims of race, class, or gender.'[4] And the entire direction of recent cultural criticism is toward a third possibility, that of 'marginalizing the center' as Abdul JanMohamed puts it,[5] by listening to minority voices and histories as *subjects* rather than as objects or simply the Other. This should not be merely a pluralism or a 'homogenization of differences',[6] but a genuine opening of the discourse so that there really are not any hegemonic parameters to it anymore. One needs, as Nancy Hartsock says, to 'build an account of the world as seen from the margins, an account which can transform these margins into centers'.[7] This whole movement in cultural studies parallels that followed by Jung's followers in relation to psychoanalysis. What relation should the stigmatized have with the stigmatizer?

Portrayed as mystics, intuitives dwelling only in the vast transpersonal dimension of existence, occultists fascinated by archaic myths and religions, are we? Then let us embrace this definition of ourselves! Let us reject any tincture of empiricism, any possible echo of the mechanistic concept of man that our stigmatizer holds. Let us organize disciples' groups that study Classical religions in depth or the various ancient mysteries that modern dreams, literature, and art seem to draw upon. Let us form quasi-religious clubs to delve further into Jung's many essays on religion.

In a way, the clash in Great Britain during the early 1940s between those Jungians who wished to preserve their Analytical Psychology Club against the encroachment of the clinically trained Jungians duplicated this process. These latter Jungians formed their own Society of Analytical Psychology as a result. The tendency of this group of Developmental Jungians is not assimilation but reintegration, with the Jungians' own distinct theoretical identity maintained: use the psychoanalytic findings that seem to bear out Jung's concept of the collective unconscious and the archetypes. Those findings are not rejected solely because of their source. More, these later Jungians have also served to draw our attention to the present actual experience of people caught in historical situations.

But the issues raised in cultural studies about the relation of the marginal voice to the central discourse have a deeper relevance than this. This direction of reintegration taken by cultural studies is the one that future Jungian studies should take also, attending to the ways in which the *marginalized* experience the process of individuation. It is very likely to differ radically from the process of those who are not marginalized, although those who are not have usually been the unquestioned subject of Jungian studies.

This may seem like an improbable direction for Jungian studies to take.

To be sure, Jung relies in his essays on evidence taken from different cultures and peoples: American Indians, Asian Indians, Melanesians, East Africans, Central Africans, West Africans, and Australian aborigines. Nor was he only the armchair anthropologist typical of ethnographers during the earlier part of this century.

In 1920 he visited North Africa, travelling through Tunis, Algeria and parts of the Sahara Desert. He felt called to return to Africa in 1925, and travelled among various tribes of Kenya and Uganda. This was not a safe and sanitary itinerary but often involved considerable danger, including one harrowing episode in which Jung and his fellow travellers joined in a tribal war-dance they were witnessing to avoid being its target.[8] In fact, Jung had a dream during this trip that he always thought later was an urgent warning from his unconscious that he was in danger of 'going black'.[9] In 1938 he visited India, both the northern and the southern states. But in his essays referring to these native peoples, written between 1916 and 1954, Jung revealed the ethnocentric bias that was characteristic of the times they were written. (1954 may seem a little late for this, but it should be remembered that Jung was then seventy-nine years old and was reflecting earlier attitudes held.) Cultures were ranked according to their level of 'civilization,' the apex being of course that of Western Europe. Jung was quite genial about this, even using this ranking to show how superior the 'primitive' peoples are to today's 'artificial' Europeans who have become cut off from their original roots. But it is painful reading today.

Thus Jung wrote in 1916: 'Primitive man has a minimum of self-awareness combined with a maximum of attachment to the object . . . All primitive magic and religion are based upon these magical attachments, which simply consist in the projection of unconscious contents upon the object.'[10] To illustrate the archetypal nature of libido-symbols, Jung wrote in 1928 of its 'primitive conception' among the Dakota, Iroquois, and Algonquin Indians, the Yaos of central Africa, the Australian aborigines, and the tribes of the 'Gold Coast'.[11] But all of these peoples are indiscriminately grouped together to illustrate how the archetypal symbol appears with a collective meaning.

In 1939 he wrote about the Asian Indian:

> The process of his thinking reminds me of the primitive way of thought-production. The primitive's reasoning is mainly an unconscious function . . . Our case was not so bad as that of the [African] Negroes or the Polynesians, who found themselves suddenly confronted with the infinitely higher civilization of the white man.[12]

And in 1954 he wrote of the Winnebago Indians' use of the trickster-myth in their religion:

> For them it still 'functions,' providing that they have not been spoiled by civilization . . . [It] points back to a very much earlier stage of consciousness which existed before

> the birth of the myth, when the Indian was still groping about in a similar mental darkness. Only when his consciousness reached a higher level could he detach the earlier state from himself and objectify it.[13]

This ethnocentrism is particularly apparent in his two essays written after his journey to India, 'The Dreamlike World of India' and 'What India Can Teach Us'.[14] Hindsight improves eyesight, but still it is rather an eerie feeling to read these 1939 essays and realize that they were written only a few years before India's War of Independence in 1947. Both unwittingly are variations on Said's theme of 'orientalism'.[15]

Thus, what Jung seemed to encounter again and again was the 'dreaminess' of timeless India which revels in the polarities of ascetic transcendence and grotesque violence because of its ancient, abiding view of spiritual life as cyclical. It is both 'highly spiritual' and 'primitive'.[16] The later reader clearly sees that what Jung was encountering was Brahmin India, always taking the 'educated Indian'[17] for all Indians. He dismissed the native Indians of lower castes as 'carry[ing] on an apparently meaningless life . . . they die and are born again in ceaseless waves, always much the same'.[18] Again and again, what he interpreted as innately Indian seems more to be what Fanon would call a 'white mask'.[19] The 'educated Indians' showed 'modesty and inconspicuousness [without any] harshness or arrogance'.[20] They had a 'peculiar obliqueness' that surely was due to their 'overcrowding'.[21] And 'in the melancholy eyes of the illiterate half-naked villager you divine an unconscious knowledge of mysterious truths'.[22] (Or a conscious knowledge of poverty, disease, and hunger.)

In the face of all this, how can one claim the present relevance of Jung's ideas for the marginalized?

For one thing, he should be given credit for his arduous and at times quite dangerous attempts made in the 1920s to reach a first-hand knowledge of native African peoples. There is a certain brave genius in joining a native war dance, shouting and stamping and cracking a rhinoceros whip, rather than remaining the white Other at a nervous distance. Further, seeking to show the similarities between native religious myths and those of Christianity may seem patronizing to some today, but then showed a serious respect for alien cultures.

As long as one is within one's history, one cannot see its underlying ideology – here, the ideology of colonialism. In 'The Dreamlike World of India,' Jung did seem aware, briefly, that the Indian colonizer did not really see the colonized as they were when he wrote: 'I did not see one European in India who really lived there. They were all living in Europe, that is, in a sort of bottle filled with European air.'[23] But then he went on to describe what India is 'really' like – and he was not a European? Still, one should look beyond Jung's outer trappings of historical bias.

For at heart, Jung's thought is quite sympathetic to the validating of all voices, marginalized or not. After all, the concept of the collective unconscious cuts across cultures and races to the underlying human experience. As Jung has frequently written, a person's present historical circumstances affect the ways in which the archetypes become manifest. Marginalized peoples have had as one of their main problems the preservation of their spiritual essence, the holding onto wholeness, as well as the maintenance of their often precarious physical life. They above all have had the very practical need of keeping a Self intact in the face of outer disintegrative forces. Archetypes aim at helping a person to do this.

Ever since its heyday in the 1970s Jungian literary criticism has faced the charge of being overly subjective, even solipsistic, in its concerns. The hero's psychological battle with an archetypal monster of the unconscious to gain a more inclusive consciousness, the heroine's mythic descent into the underworld to achieve the chthonic wisdom of the earth-goddess, the night sea journey of either to reach a spiritual rebirth, all were familiar themes that the Jungian critic found in literature. All showed an absorption with the individual as a monad.

Jung may have written: 'Individuation does not shut one out from the world, but gathers the world to oneself[24] . . .

There arises a consciousness which is no longer imprisoned in the petty, oversensitive, personal world of the ego, but participates freely in the wider world of objective interests . . . The individual [is brought] into absolute, binding, and indissoluble communion with the world at large.'[25] But his literary followers have tended to see individuation as a quest inwards toward an understanding of the unconscious that leads to an expanded self-knowledge.

The unspoken and unexamined assumptions of this criticism exclude any consideration of the marginalized experience. All – writer, reader, and critic – are assumed to share a process of individuation that is not scarred or deformed by a social evaluation of oneself as being innately inferior. Participation in the hegemony is taken for granted.

A good example of this is a recent publication by one of the most prolific of Jungian literary critics, Bettina L. Knapp, that purports to be *A Jungian Approach to Literature.*[26] Works of the world literature from all time-periods are used to illustrate the various elements of Jungian theory such as the Hero archetype, the Anima archetype, the Individuation process, and so on. The 'approach' consists of an 'archetypal analysis [that] takes the literature out of the individual . . . context and relates it to humankind in general'. This criticism will help readers to see that their particular problems are really timeless, and that 'their reality is part of an ongoing and cyclical reality'.[27]

This kind of therapeutic 'Jungian approach' is so familiar from the old myth-criticism days that it may seem scarcely worth remarking. But the book was published in 1984. What of all the seismic critical shifts that had occurred by that time? Should not such an 'approach' take these into account somehow?

As is quite characteristic of Jungian literary criticism, there is the supposition here that any social prejudice in the specific cultural context of the reader or writer is irrelevant to the 'archetypal analysis'. Thus, as is also characteristic, all of the writers she examines are white males and either of the middle or upper class, save for the Sufi Attar who certainly was of the elite.

This was true of the rest of Jungian literary criticism of the 1960s and 1970s.[28] In his definitive bibliography of Jungian literary criticism, Jos Van Meurs lists 902 entries dating from 1920 to the mid-1980s. Tellingly, only four entries are critical analyses of African-American writers, and those the crossover authors who are now part of the African-American canon: Maya Angelou, James Baldwin, Ralph Ellison, LeRoi Jones, and Toni Morrison.[29] It is clear both from the annotations in his bibliography and from his overview that the question of how the writers' cultural context might have shaped those myths and archetypes is not considered by any of the critics. The studies from the beginning onward have dealt with writers who were usually male, usually European, and almost always white. Of course, this has also been a blind-spot of criticism more generally until quite recently. Still, other schools of criticism have not claimed to give insight into the collective experience of humanity.

But a culture may make individual individuation quite difficult, that is obvious. How is the Jungian literary critic to factor in the minority person's very immediate experience of cultural victimizing and dissociation? The methodology of New Historicism may help here for it assumes that every time-period has its blind spots, its ideology that seems 'transparent' to those who participate in the dominant culture. Those archetypes that are present in minority literature could point to these blind spots, compensating as archetypes do for problems and conflicts in the individual's conscious life.

Recently, Shelburne has reminded us of the importance of 'cultural influence' in the 'phenomenological form of the archetypal images'.[30] Evelyn J. Hinz and John J. Teunissen also consider the influence of the historical frame upon archetypes. Archetypes may be timeless and connect all people to the collective unconscious. But it is the 'interaction between this extrahistorical force and the temporal' that gives a literary work its power, creating a sense in writer and reader of 'the otherwordly, of the divine'.[31] They go on to postulate as an 'axiom' that 'just as the archetype cannot be contained in its individual manifestation – its temporary location – so neither can it be . . . observed independently of the frame in which it manifests itself.'[32]

The underlying archetypal level is what all peoples share, no matter what their places in society. But the effects of being socially marginalized may affect the way that archetypes are known by the individual. A Jungian analysis of such individuals should take into account this factor of marginalization, as the Jungian critic should do when studying the literature of such people.

It may well be that in this literature, archetypal symbols more often function in their positive, healing role as reminders of the possibility of wholeness. The 'cultural influence' may be the most salient point to consider. There could be the person's internalization of the outer denial of value, or what Yeats has called:

> That defiling and disfigured shape
> The mirror of malicious eyes
> Casts upon his eyes until at last
> He thinks that shape must be his shape.
> ('Dialogue of Self and Soul', lines 52–5)

Or there could be a conscious assimilation into the majority group because of a denial of one's own minority people. Archetypes may help to restore wholeness by drawing the one who feels dwindled and separated from the society through no personal fault back into the collective experience. Jung has warned against possible dangers of the 'identification with the collective psyche', namely a state of 'godlikeness'.[33] But still, there may be somewhat different dangers for those who society has defined as being 'ungodlike' in essence. Archetypes with their numinosity above all can be power-giving and power-restoring.

There are some Jungian literary critics who have begun to use analytical psychology to study how the writer's marginal state may be answered by the archetypal symbols in the literary work, and how the cultural context of this writer may result in the recurrence of certain archetypes. These are the increasing numbers of critics who work with

Jungian psychology to study literature written by women.[34]

And indeed, this is a promising beginning for such a future Jungian literary criticism, fulfilling as it does the challenge to 'build an account of the world as seen from the margins, an account which can transform these margins into centers'.[35] One might take this even further, into a feminist metacriticism that analyzes the psychological meaning of contemporary feminist criticism itself. Feminist critics might examine more closely the strong interest in the pre-Oedipal mother that prevails in current feminist criticism.

No matter what the ideological persuasion, the critic is very frequently drawn to this hitherto unexplored possibility of an archaic time before Logos, or rational language, when the mother dominates. It is the 'excav[ation] of that shadowy Minoan culture'[36] in which 'feminists . . . begin to speak our mother tongue'.[37] The feminist critic wishes to study the re-capturing of this time of fusion, not only the figure of the mother.

Of course, the object-relations theory of the pre-Oedipal period that such critics employ, and ego psychology generally, assume the possibility of an adult ego, or unified self, being formed. As Martha Noel Evans says with succinct irony:

> Men may undermine mastery and valorize nonmastery, but they do so in the mode of those who have known from the inside what mastery may be. [Women writers] hardly need to explore the territory of nonmastery, for they already know it too well . . . While the character of women's writing, with its projects of self-definition and achievement of authority, gives the impression of being naive, simplistic, or behind the times, it is in fact already on the far side of the postmodernist project.[38]

Feminist studies of gender difference very often involve the figure of the mother. Stanton has studied the metaphor of the maternal in the writings of Kristeva, Irigiray, and Cixous, but does so to warn us that this 'valorization of the maternal–feminine' may well 'congeal as feminine essence'.[39] But one might consider this 'metaphor' as signaling something else. Again and again in this French criticism of *l'écriture féminine,* the archetype of the Great Mother appears in different guises with her 'cherishing and nourishing goodness, her orgiastic emotionality, and her Stygian depths'.[40]

In *This Sex Which Is Not One,* Irigiray connects women's sexuality with the way in which she uses language (*parler femme,* as Irigiray calls it): multiple voices, fluid syntax, circular rather than linear structure, openness rather than closure. Cixous more clearly evokes this archetype, often in the elevated style that accompanies such symbols. This may seen in its purest form in 'The Laugh of the Medusa'. There she says of the woman writer: 'There is always within her at least a little of that good mother's milk. She writes in white ink.'[41]

We should recall that the Great Mother is the feminine archetype of the Self, and then consider how this symbol might be functioning in this criticism. The French interest in *l'écriture féminine* grew primarily as a reaction to the enormous influence of Lacan's theory of language and what many considered his privileging of the phallus as symbolic of the Law of the Father that dominates culture. These French feminists with their almost defiant panegyrics of *l'écriture féminine* answer the Lacanian theory of woman's 'lack' of phallus (*manqué* is his term) by proclaiming the man's lack of yoni. They summon up the Great Mother archetype to remind the woman of her potential wholeness in the face of dissociation, that is the Freudian and Lacanian definition of woman as negation, as 'lack'.

The response to this French feminist criticism by their female readers is nearly always a delighted glee, as even their hostile critics admit. Stanton, for example, originally praised such writing in her 1980 essay, and although she came to criticize it five years later she still admitted that it has 'an inspiring, empowering value of women'.[42] And why exactly should the reminder of the power of one's essence, the summoning of this archetype of the unified

Self, be 'fatal to constructive political action'? It would seem to be prior to any such agenda. Social conditions cannot change until the person they oppress is strong enough to change them, no longer defining herself as the oppressor defines her and unwilling to tolerate his conditions any longer.

So feminist literary critics might consider the persistent appearance in their works of the Great Mother, particularly in her chthonic aspect, no matter how unwelcome or ideologically suspect she is. What does this presence portend for the future of gender criticism? Such critics might also reflect on the possible implications of the strong pull toward the primal and the archetypal that may be felt in many of the studies on difference, for it really seems to be a pull toward essence.

However, these critics still only deal with the one marginal group, women. More specifically, they deal with white women. But what of women of color? As such women have been reminding the feminist movement as a whole in increasingly strident tones, *their* situation and *their* concerns are not necessarily or even usually the same as those of white women. Consider, for example, Barbara Christian's acid dismissal of 'the French feminist theorists' (by whom she presumably means Irigiray, Kristeva and Cixous) for their 'tendency toward monolithism' in ignoring women of other races and ethnic groups when they presume to speak for all women.[43] Once again, those of the majority group are taking their experience to be that of all other groups.

What other direction might future Jungian literary criticism take?

It could begin by considering common features that minority cultures share due to their marginal place within their societies at large. Memmi has analyzed the usual tendency for colonized peoples to seek to strengthen their communal identity by immersing themselves in the traditional family structure.[44] Such a family provides a sustaining, nourishing support that counteracts the individual's despair in the face of outer social negation, and it also ensures that the minority group will continue with its traditional identity and values enduring and intact. Central to this structure is the time-honored, one may even say archetypal, role that the mother plays in nurturing and preserving family identity. And it is apparent that in many minority cultures the mother is a powerful figure, even if the woman as such is not.

This could be a possible way of entry into an archetypal study of the marginalized for the Jungian critic, who could use in particular the findings of the Developmental Jungians. For if the mother plays such an important role in preserving cultural identity, then presumably that archetype will also be prominent in marginalized literatures.

Along with this, Memmi notes the dual role of the family in maintaining cultural identity: it nurtures the individual but it can also smother and devour. As he says about the 'potential rebel' who seeks refuge in the traditional family: 'For the young man [now, we would add "woman" as well], it is an internal catastrophe. He will remain glued to that family which offers him warmth and tenderness but which simultaneously absorbs, clutches and emasculates him.'[45] The Mother archetype also can assume this polar appearance for the individual.

If the mother usually is an important figure in marginalized cultures, so quite often is the sense of exaggerated maleness known as machismo. Machismo provokes such strong negative and positive responses and has so many practical repercussions that an analysis of its archetypal function seems long overdue. For machismo seems like a manifestation of the Wise Old Man archetype, albeit in a negative, distorted form.

Jung says of the Wise Old Man archetype that is the archetype of Self for men:

> The wise old man appears . . . in the guise of a magician, doctor, priest . . . grandfather, or any other person possessing authority. The archetype of spirit in the shape of a man . . . always appears in a situation where insight, understanding, good advice, determination, planning, etc., are needed but cannot be mustered on one's own

> resources. The archetype compensates this state of spiritual deficiency by contents designed to fill the gap.[46]

It may well be that the machismo that is so widespread among the men of oppressed cultures – most notably African-Americans and Latinos – may represent the felt absence of any positive experience of this male archetype of the Self, denied to these men by their outer societies.

Somehow machismo seems complementary to the archetypal pull of the mother, a defensive attitude aimed at preserving the Self. The alternative attitude to the macho male seems to be his yielding to the devaluation of Self that the society at large has assigned to him.

This reading of machismo as a manifestation of the Wise Old Man archetype is reinforced by the closer look at the African-American male attitude of 'coolness' that is given by Richard Majors and Janet Mancini Billson.[47] They describe at length the emotional costs of the 'cool pose', from the avoidance of intimacy to the problems of the rising rate of illegitimacy, crime, and violence. But they also trace the 'cool pose' to slavery days and before, when such a pose was essential to survival. The 'spiritual meaning' of coolness is 'the sense of control, symmetry, correct presentation of self, and sophistication'.[48] It was known as *ashe* in ancient Nigerian society and, imported to American slave-plantations, became a way of enduring the widespread degradation of slavery.[49] A great many black men today still know the degradation of racism and the denial of their intrinsic worth. Indeed the machismo of 'coolness' seems related to the Wise Old Man archetype.

Thus the whole field of cultural studies may revitalize Jungian literary criticism, and help to bring it forward into present poststructuralist times. For if the function of archetypal symbols differs for the marginalized person, then those symbols probably take other forms with other meanings than they do in the literature of writers belonging to the 'central' society. The archetypes of Self for men and for women – the Wise Old Man and the Chthonic Mother – particularly may vary in function and form. In connection with this, the later Developmental Jungians should be studied in greater depth. One should listen to what they have to say.

But before one can do this, one must first listen to what Jung himself has to say.

Notes

PART I INTRODUCTION

1. Sigmund Freud, *Standard Edition of the Complete Psychological Works,* tr. James Strachey (London: Hogarth Press, 1953) vol. 13, p.18.
2. Ibid., p. 33.

1 THE BANNED VOICE

1. William McGuire (ed.), *The Freud/Jung Letters: The Correspondence Between Sigmund Freud and C.G. Jung,* tr. Ralph Manheim and R.F.C. Hull (Princeton: Princeton University Press, 1974).
2. C.G. Jung, *Memories, Dreams, Reflections,* Aniela Jaffé (ed.) (New York: Random House, 1961) p. 155.
3. *The Freud/Jung Letters,* p. 216.
4. Ibid., p. 220.
5. Ibid., p. 217.
6. Ibid., p. 218.
7. Ibid., p. 220
8. Ibid., p. 201.
9. See Jeffrey Moussaieff Masson, *The Assault on Truth: Freud's Suppression of the Seduction Theory* (New York: Farrar, Straus & Giroux, 1984), especially his comments on pages 2–4.
10. *The Freud/Jung Letters,* p. 121, p. 136, p. 169, p. 209.
11. Ibid., p. 209.
12. Ibid., pp. 211–12
13. Ibid., p. 216.
14. Ibid., pp. 225–6.
15. Ibid., pp. 251–2.
16. Paul E. Stepansky, *In Freud's Shadow: Adler in Context* (Hillsdale, NJ: Analytic Press, 1983) p. 100.

17. *The Freud/Jung Letters,* p. 308.
18. Ibid., p. 310.
19. Ibid., p. 421.
20. Ibid., p. 421n.
21. Ibid., p. 422.
22. Ibid., p. 427.
23. Ibid., p. 429.
24. Peter Gay, *Freud: A Life For Our Time* (New York: Norton, 1988) p. 58.
25. Ernest Jones, *The Life and Work of Sigmund Freud,* vol. 2, *Years of Maturity 1901–19* (New York: Basic Books, 1957) p. 140.
26. Freud, *Standard Edition,* vol. 17, pp. 217–52.
27. Ibid., p. 220.
28. *The Freud/Jung Letters,* p. 472.
29. Ibid., p. 474.
30. Ibid., p. 475.
31. Ibid., p. 476.
32. Ibid., p. 476.
33. Ibid., p. 479.
34. Ibid., p. 481.
35. Ibid., p. 483.
36. Ibid., p. 483.
37. Ibid., pp. 483–4.
38. Ibid., pp. 484–5.
39. Ibid., p. 487.
40. Ibid., pp. 488–9.
41. Ibid., pp. 490–1.
42. Ibid., p. 492.
43. Ibid., p. 493.
44. Ibid., p. 500.
45. Ibid., p. 502.
46. Ibid., p. 503.
47. Ibid., pp. 505–6.
48. Ibid., p. 507.
49. Ibid., p. 508.
50. Ibid., p. 510.
51. Ibid., p. 511.
52. Jones, *The Life and Work of Freud,* vol. 2, p. 33.
53. Gay, *Freud: A Life For Our Time,* p. 230.
54. *The Freud/Jung Letters,* p. 514.
55. Ibid., p. 514n.
56. Gay, *Freud: A Life For Our Time,* p. 231.

57. *The Freud/Jung Letters*, pp. 515–16.
58. Ibid., p. 521.
59. Ibid., p. 522.
60. Ibid., pp. 523–4.
61. Ibid., pp. 526–7.
62. Ibid., pp. 531–2.
63. Ibid., p. 533.
64. Ibid., p. 533.
65. Ibid., pp. 534–5.
66. Ibid., p. 537.
67. Ibid., pp. 539–40.
68. Ibid., p. 539.
69. Ibid., p. 540.
70. Freud, *Standard Edition*, vol. 13, pp. 18–20.
71. Ibid., pp. 20–22.
72. Francois Roustang, *Dire Mastery: Discipleship from Freud to Lacan*, tr. by Ned Lukacher (Baltimore: Johns Hopkins University Press, 1982, orig. pub. 1976) p. 51.
73. Reuben Fine, *A History of Psychoanalysis* (New York: Columbia University Press, 1979) p. 86. In his expanded edition of 1990, he makes the same estimations of Jung.
74. John Gedo, *Conceptual Issues in Psychoanalysis: Essays in History and Method* (Hillsdale, NJ: Analytic Press, 1986) p. 35.
75. Gay, *Freud: A Life For Our Time*, p. 311.
76. Jay Greenberg and Stephen Mitchell, *Object Relations in Psychoanalytic Theory* (Cambridge, MA, and London: Harvard University Press, 1983) p. 79.
77. Gay, *Freud: A Life For Our Time*, p. 759.
78. Juliet Mitchell, *Psychoanalysis and Feminism: Freud, Reich, Laing, and Women* (New York: Random House, 1974) p. 318.
79. Judith Kegan Gardiner, 'Mind Mother: Psychoanalysis and Feminism,' in *Making A Difference: Feminist Literary Criticism*, Gayle Green and Coppèlia Kahn (ed.) (London: Methuen, 1985) p. 124.
80. Ellie Ragland-Sullivan, *Jacques Lacan and the Philosophy of Psychoanalysis* (Urbana, IL: University of Illinois Press, 1986) p. 100.
81. Ibid., p. 185.
82. Robert S. Wallerstein, 'One Psychoanalysis or Many?' *International Journal of Psychoanalysis* 69 (1988), p. 5.
83. Ibid., pp. 5–6.
84. Ibid., p. 12.

85. Ibid., p. 13.
86. Adolf Grünbaum, *The Foundation of Psychoanalysis: A Philosophical Critique* (Berkeley, Los Angeles, and London: University of California Press, 1984).
87. Donald P. Spence, *The Freudian Metaphor: Toward Paradigm Change in Psychoanalysis* (New York: Norton, 1987).
88. In this connection, see especially pp. 73–7 in his chapter, 'The Metaphor of Psychoanalysis as a Science.'
89. Riccardo Steiner, 'Die Weltmachtstellung der Britischen Reichs: Notes on the Term "Standard" in the First Translation of Freud,' in *Freud in Exile: Psychoanalysis and Its Vicissitudes,* Edward Timms and Naomi Segal (ed.) (New Haven and London: Yale University Press, 1988), pp. 184–5.
90. Ibid., p. 187.
91. Ibid., p. 188.
92. Helmut Junker, 'On Difficulties of Retranslating Freud into English: Reading Experiences of a German Analyst,' in *Freud in Exile.*
93. Bruno Bettelheim, *Freud and Man's Soul* (New York: Knopf, 1982).
94. Darius Gray Ornston, Jr, 'How Standard is the "Standard Edition"?' in *Freud in Exile,* pp. 196–7.
95. Emmett Wilson, 'Did Strachey Invent Freud?' *International Review of Psychoanalysis* 14 (1987), pp. 299–315.
96. Ibid., p. 300.

2 APPROPRIATION

1. William McGuire, (ed.), *The Freud/Jung Letters: The Correspondence Between Sigmund Freud and C.G. Jung,* tr. Ralph Manheim and R.F.C. Hull (Princeton: Princeton University Press, 1974) pp. 251–2.
2. Ibid., p. 255.
3. Ibid., p. 258.
4. Ibid., p. 258.
5. Ibid., p. 259.
6. Ibid., p. 260.
7. Ibid., p. 260.
8. Ibid., p. 263.

9. Ibid., p. 264.
10. Ibid., p. 265.
11. Ibid., p. 258.
12. Ibid., p. 269.
13. Ibid., p. 276.
14. Ibid., p. 277.
15. Ibid., p. 279.
16. Ibid., p. 279.
17. Ibid., p. 282.
18. Peter Gay, *Freud: A life For Our Time* (New York: Norton, 1988) p. 227.
19. Ibid., p. 324.
20. Ibid., pp. 324–5.
21. *The Freud/Jung Letters*, p. 285.
22. Ibid., p. 288n.
23. Ibid., pp. 288–9.
24. Ibid., p. 298.
25. Ibid., p. 320.
26. Ibid., p. 326.
27. Ibid., p. 326.
28. Ibid., p. 328
29. Ibid., p. 332.
30. Ibid., p. 335.
31. Ibid., p. 336.
32. Ibid., p. 337.
33. Ibid., p. 335.
34. Ibid., p. 336.
35. Ibid., p. 337.
36. Ibid., p. 378.
37. Ibid., p. 384.
38. Ibid., p. 388.
39. Ibid., p. 422.
40. Ibid., p. 427.
41. Ibid., p. 429.
42. Ibid., p. 438.
43. Ibid., p. 439.
44. Ibid., p. 441.
45. Ibid., p. 443.
46. Ibid., p. 449.
47. Ibid., p. 450.
48. Ibid., p. 459.
49. Fliess wrote to Freud in 1904: 'I have come across a book by Weininger in the first biological part of which I find, to my

consternation, a description of my ideas on bisexuality and the nature of sexual attraction consequent upon it – feminine men attract masculine women and vice versa. From a quotation in it I see that Weininger knew Swoboda – your pupil – [before the publication of the book] . . . . I have no doubt that Weininger obtained knowledge of my ideas via you and misused someone else's property. What do you know about it?' *The Complete Letters of Sigmund Freud to Wilhelm Fliess, 1887–1904*, tr. Jeffrey Moussaieff Masson (ed.) (Cambridge: Harvard University Press, 1985) p. 463.

50. Ibid., p. 464.
51. Ibid., p. 465.
52. Ibid., p. 466.
53. *The Freud/Jung Letters*, p. 460.
54. Ibid., p. 469.
55. Ibid., p. 255.
56. Ibid., p. 480.
57. Ibid., p. 483.
58. Ibid., p. 485.
59. Ibid., p. 486.
60. Ibid., p. 487.
61. Ibid., p. 472.
62. Sigmund Freud, *Standard Edition of the Complete Psychological Works*, tr. James Strachey (London: Hogarth Press, 1953) vol. 13, p. xiii.
63. Ibid., *The Freud/Jung Letters*, p. 258.
64. Ibid., p. 269.
65. Ibid., pp. 288–9.
66. Freud, *Standard Edition*, vol. 13, p. 1.
67. Ibid., p. 31.
68. Ibid., p. 66.
69. Freud, *Standard Edition*, vol. 14, p. 35.
70. Ibid., p. 35.
71. Ibid., p. 36.
72. Ibid., p. 36.
73. Ibid., p. 37
74. Freud, 'Obsessional Actions and Religious Practices' in *Standard Edition*, vol. 9.
75. C.G. Jung, *The Psychogenesis of Mental Diseases* (Princeton: Princeton University Press, 1960).
76. Freud, *Standard Edition*, vol. 14, p. 30.
77. Ibid., pp. 29–30.

78. C.G. Jung, *The Structure and Dynamics of the Psyche* (Princeton: Princeton University Press, 1960; 2nd edn. 1969) pp. 96–101.
79. C.G. Jung, *The Archetypes and the Collective Unconscious* (Princeton: Princeton University Press, 1959; 2nd edn, 1968) p. 164.
80. C.G. Jung, *Psychological Types* (Princeton: Princeton University Press, 1921, pub. 1971) p. v.
81. C.G. Jung, *Memories, Dreams, Reflections,* Aniela Jaffé (ed.) (New York: Random House, 1961) p. 207.
82. Freud, *Standard Edition,* vol. 17, p. 245.
83. Andrew Samuels, *Jung and the Post-Jungians* (London, Boston, Melbourne & Henley: Routledge & Kegan Paul, 1985) pp. 9–11.
84. Ibid., pp. 10–11.

3 EXCLUSION

1. R. Andrew Paskauskas, 'The Jones-Freud Era, 1908–1939,' in *Freud in Exile: Psychoanalysis and Its Vicissitudes,* Edward Timms and Naomi Segal (ed.) (New Haven and London: Yale University Press, 1988) p. 114.
2. Ibid., p. 118.
3. Jeffrey Moussaieff Masson, *The Assault on Truth: Freud's Suppression of the Seduction Theory* (New York: Farrar, Straus & Giroux, 1984) p. 173.
4. Ibid., p. 174.
5. Ibid., p. 152.
6. Ibid., pp. 283–95.
7. Ernest Jones, *The Life and Work of Sigmund Freud,* Vol.2, *Years of Maturity 1901–1919* (New York: Basic Books, 1957) p. 83.
8. Jeffrey Moussaieff Masson, tr. (ed.), *The Complete Letters of Sigmund Freud to Wilhelm Fliess, 1887–1904* (Cambridge: Harvard University Press, 1985) p. 11.
9. Ibid., pp. 11–12.
10. Masson, *The Assault on Truth,* p. xvii.
11. Ibid., pp. 114–19.
12. Ibid., pp. 117–18.
13. Paul Roazen, *Encountering Freud: The Politics and Histories of Psychoanalysis* (New Brunswick, NJ, and London: Transaction Press, 1990) p. xiv.

14. Paul Roazen, *Freud and his Followers* (New York: Knopf, 1975) p. 224.
15. Ibid., p. 224.
16. William McGuire, (ed.), *The Freud/Jung Letters: The Correspondence Between Sigmund Freud and C.G. Jung*, tr. Ralph Manheim and R.F.C. Hull (Princeton: Princeton University Press, 1974) p. xxiii.
17. Ibid., p. 289.
18. Ibid., p. 291.
19. Roazen, *Encountering Freud*, p. xiv.
20. Raymond Dyer, *Her Father's Daughter: the Work of Anna Freud* (New York: Aronson Press, 1983) p. 26.
21. Elisabeth Young-Bruhel, *Anna Freud: A Biography* (New York: Summit Press, 1988) p. 80.
22. Maud Bodkin, *Archetypal Patterns in Poetry: Psychological Studies of Imagination* (London: Oxford University Press, 1951).
23. Northrop Frye, *Anatomy of Criticism: Four Essays* (Princeton: Princeton University Press, 1957).
24. C.G. Jung, *The Structure and Dynamics of the Psyche* (Princeton: Princeton University Press, 1960; 2nd edn, 1969); *The Archetypes and the Collective Unconscious* (Princeton: Princeton University Press, 1959; 2nd edn, 1968); *Aion: Researches into the Phenomenology of the Self* (Princeton: Princeton University Press, 1958; 2nd edn, 1968); and *Psychology and Religion: West and East* (Princeton: Princeton University Press, 1958; 2nd edn, 1969).
25. Frank Lentricchia, *After the New Criticism* (Chicago: University of Chicago Press, 1980) p. 124.
26. Edith Kurzweil, *The Age of Structuralism: Lévi-Strauss to Foucault* (New York: Columbia University Press, 1980).
27. Ibid., p.i.
28. Ibid., p. 11n.
29. Ibid., p. 14.
30. Ibid., p. 237.
31. Paul Kugler, 'The Unconscious in a Postmodern Depth Psychology,' in *C.G. Jung and the Humanities*, Karin Barnby and Pellegrino D'Acierno (eds.) (Princeton: Princeton University Press, 1990) pp. 310–1.
32. C. G. Jung, *The Spirit in Man, Art, and Literature* (Princeton: Princeton University Press, 1966) p. 100.
33. Ibid., p. 95.

34. Ibid., pp. 96–7.
35. Ibid., p. 101.
36. Ibid., p. 112.
37. Ibid., p. 135, p. 140.
38. C.G Jung, *Symbols of Transformation* (Princeton: Princeton University Press, 1956; 2nd edn, 1967) pp. 313–37.
39. Ibid., p. 313.
40. Jung, *Archetypes*, p. 28, p. 30, p. 71, p. 200, and p. 285.
41. Sigmund Freud, *Standard Edition of the Complete Psychological Works*, tr. James Strachey (London: Hogarth Press, 1953) vol. 9, p. 54.
42. Freud, 'The Theme of the Three Caskets,' in *Standard Edition*, vol. 12.
43. Freud, *Standard Edition*, vol. 17, p. 227.
44. Freud, 'Dostoevsky and Parricide,' in *Standard Edition*, vol. 21, p. 184.
45. Jung, 'Answer to Job,' in *Psychology and Religion.*
46. Ibid., p. 404.
47. Ibid., pp. 440–1.
48. So see Robert N. Mollinger's Bibliography in *Psychoanalysis and Literature: an Introduction* (Chicago: Nelson-Hall, 1981) p. 169; and Elizabeth Wright's References in *Psychoanalytic Criticism: Theory in Practice* (London: Methuen Press, 1984) p. 186.
49. Mollinger, *Psychoanalysis and Literature*, pp. 62–3.
50. Ibid., p. 62.
51. Edith Kurzweil and William Phillips (eds.), *Literature and Psychoanalysis* (New York: Columbia University Press, 1983) p. vii.
52. Ibid., p. 3.
53. Wright, *Psychoanalytic Criticism*, p. 76.
54. Ibid., p. 70.
55. Shirley F. Straton (ed.), *Literary Theories in Praxis* (Philadelphia: University of Pennsylvania Press, 1987) p. 97.
56. Ibid., p. 97.
57. Eric Gould, *Mythical Intentions in Modern Literature* (Princeton: Princeton University Press, 1981).
58. Ibid., p. 37.
59. Ibid., p. 23.
60. Mollinger, *Psychoanalysis and Literature*, pp. 61–3.
61. Ibid., p. 63.
62. Wright, *Psychoanalytic Criticism*, p. 69.

63. Ibid., p. 70.
64. Paul Kugler, in Norman Holland, *Holland's Guide to Psychoanalytic Psychology and Literature-and-Psychology* (New York: Oxford University Press, 1990) pp. 42–3.
65. Ibid., p. 37.
66. If Jung has been useful primarily to the myth-critics of the 1960s and 1970s, it is the revisionist post-Jungian James Hillman who seems to have captured the attention of later literary critics, most them feminist in orientation. More will be said about Hillman in Chapters 4 and 5. For the works of such critics, see: Barbara Charlesworth Gelpi, 'The Politics of Androgyny,' *Women's Studies* 2, no. 2 (1974) pp. 151–60; Naomi Goldenberg, 'A Feminist Critique of Jung,' *Signs* 2, no. 2 (1976), pp. 443–9; Estella Lauter and Carol Schreier Rupprecht (eds), *Feminist Archetypal Theory* (Knoxville: University of Tennessee, 1985); Carol Schreier Rupprecht, 'Enlightening Shadows: Between Feminism and Archetypalism,' in *C.G. Jung and the Humanities: Toward a Hermeneutics of Culture*, Karin Baraby and Pellegrino D'Acierno (eds) (Princeton: Princeton University Press, 1990); Jos Van Meurs, 'A Survey of Jungian Literary Criticism in English,' in *Jung and the Humanities*, p. 248; Ralph Maud, 'Archetypal Depth Criticism and Melville,' *College English* 45, no. 7 (1983), pp. 695–704; and David Tacey, *Patrick White: Fiction and the Unconscious* (Melborne and New York: Oxford University Press, 1988).
67. Kugler in *Holland's Guide*, p. 43.
68. David L. Miller, 'An Other Jung and An Other. . .' in *Jung and the Humanities*, p. 325.
69. Ibid., p. 327.
70. Ibid., p. 332.

PART II INTRODUCTION

1. Mary Douglas, *Purity and Danger: An Analysis of Concepts of Pollution and Taboo* (New York: Praeger, 1966) pp. 97, 112–13.
2. Ibid., p. 97.
3. See Douglas, particularly chapters, 'Secular Defilement' and 'The Abominations of Leviticus.'
4. Ibid., p. 2.

5. C. G. Jung, *Memories, Dreams, Reflections,* Aniela Jaffé (ed.) (New York, Random House, 1961) p. 150.
6. Ibid., pp. 5–6.
7. Donald Spence, *The Freudian Metaphor: Toward Paradigm Change in Psychoanalysis* (New York: Norton, 1987).
8. Ibid., pp. 73–4.
9. Ibid., p. 75.
10. Douglas, *Purity and Danger,* p. 113.

4 MARGINALITY AND POWER

1. Henri F. Ellenberger, *The Discovery of the Unconscious: The History and Evolution of Dynamic Psychiatry* (New York: Basic Books, 1970) pp. 447, 670–3.
2. C.G. Jung, *Memories, Dreams, Reflections,* Aniela Jaffé (ed.) (New York: Random House, 1961) p. 170.
3. Peter Homans, *Jung in Context: Modernity and the Making of a Psychology* (Chicago: University of Chicago Press, 1979) p. 87.
4. Ibid., pp. 74–114.
5. Francois Roustang, *Dire Mastery: Discipleship from Freud to Lacan.* tr. Ned Lukacher (Baltimore: Johns Hopkins University Press, 1982, orig. pub. 1976) pp. 36–54.
6. Jung, *Memories,* chapter heading for pp. 170–99.
7. Ibid., p. 189.
8. Ibid., p. 193.
9. Ibid., pp. 176–7.
10. Ibid., pp. 178–9.
11. Ibid., pp. 378–90.
12. Ibid., pp. 190–1.
13. The first two essays are contained in the Appendices of C.G. Jung's *Two Essays on Analytical Psychology* (Princeton: Princeton University Press, 1953, 2nd edn. 1966) pp. 245–304, and the third, pp. 227–41 in the same volume.
14. Ibid., pp. 282–3.
15. Ibid., p. 287.
16. Ibid., p. 282.
17. Ibid., p. 299.
18. Ibid., p. 300.
19. Ibid., pp. 273–8.

20. Ibid., p. 233.
21. Ibid., p. 233.
22. Ibid., p. 234.
23. Ibid., p. 235.
24. Ibid., p. 171.
25. For a good discussion of Jung's typology, see Mary Ann Mattoon, *Jungian Psychology in Perspective* (New York: The Free Press, Macmillan, 1981) pp. 53–82.
26. Ibid., p. 81.
27. Jung, *Two Essays*, p. 80.
28. Ibid., p. 40.
29. C. G. Jung, *Aion: Researches Into the Phenomenology of the Self* (Princeton: Princeton University Press, 1959, 2nd edn. 1968).
30. Ibid., p. 3.
31. See 'The Effects of the Unconscious Upon Consciousness' in Jung, *Two Essays*, especially the chapters 'Phenomena Resulting from the Assimilation of the Unconscious' and 'Negative Attempts to Free the Individuality from the Collective Psyche'.
32. Jung, *Two Essays*, p. 138; and C.G. Jung, *The Structure and Dynamics of the Psyche* (Princeton: Princeton University Press, 1960, 2nd edn. 1969) p. 226.
33. Jung, *Two Essays*, p. 138.
34. Jung, *Structure*, pp. 137–8.
35. Ibid., pp. 227–8.
36. Ibid., p. 227.
37. Ibid., p. 158.
38. C.G. Jung, *The Archetypes and the Collective Unconscious* (Princeton: Princeton University Press, 1959, 2nd edn. 1968) p. 43.
39. Jung, *Structure*, p. 97.
40. Ibid., p. 94.
41. Ibid., p. 101.
42. Jung, *Archetypes*, p. 42.
43. Ibid., p. 48.
44. Walter A. Shelburne, *Mythos and Logos in the Thought of Carl Jung: The Theory of the Collective Unconscious in Scientific Perspective* (Albany, NY: State University of New York Press, 1988) p. 33.
45. Jung, *Two Essays*, p. 177.
46. Ibid., p. 173.
47. Jung, *Structure*, p. 226.

48. Ibid., p. 209.
49. C.G. Jung *Psychological Types* (Princeton: Princeton University Press, 1921, pub. 1971) p. ix.
50. C.G. Jung, *The Practice of Psychotherapy* (Princeton: Princeton University Press, 1954, 2nd edn. 1966).
51. Sigmund Freud, *The Standard Edition of the Complete Psychological Works*, tr. James Strachey (London: Hogarth Press, 1957) vol. 13, p. xiii.
52. Andrew Samuels, *Jung and the Post-Jungians* (London: Routledge & Kegan Paul, 1985).
53. Jung, *Two Essays*, p. 170.
54. Michael Fordham, *Jungian Psychotherapy: A Study in Analytical Psychology* (Chichester and New York: Wiley, 1978) pp. 50–1.
55. Samuels, p. 47.
56. So see Estella Lauter and Carol Schreier Rupprecht, (eds), *Feminist Archetypal Theory: Interdisciplinary Re-Visions of Jungian Thought* (Knoxville: University of Tennessee Press, 1985) pp. 10–11; and Paul Kugler, pp. 36–7 in Norman Holland, *Holland's Guide to Psychoanalytic Psychology and Literature-and-Psychology* (New York: Oxford University Press, 1990).
57. James Hillman, *Archetypal Psychology: A Brief Account* (Dallas, Texas: Spring Publications, 1983) p. 1.
58. Samuels, pp. 241–2.
59. Ibid., p. 241.
60. Ibid., pp. 46–7.
61. Hillman, p. 5.
62. Samuels, p. 244.
63. Hillman, p. 16.
64. Samuels, p. 241.
65. Shelburne, p. 83.
66. Ibid., p. 84.
67. Ibid., p. 85.
68. Gerhard Adler, 'Methods of Treatment in Analytical Psychology,' in *Psychoanalytic Techniques: A Handbook for the Practicing Psychoanalyst*, Benjamin B. Wolman (ed.) (New York: Basic Books, 1967) pp. 339–40.
69. Fordham, *Jungian Psychotherapy*, p. 53.
70. Ernest Jones, *The Life and Work of Sigmund Freud*, Vol. 3, *The Last Phase, 1919–1939* (New York: Basic Books, 1957) p. 218.
71. Ibid., p. 221.

72. Ibid., p. 226.
73. Pearl King, 'Early Divergences between the Psycho-Analytical Societies in London and Vienna,' in *Freud in Exile: Psychoanalysis and Its Vicissitudes*, Edward Timms and Naomi Segal (eds.) (New Haven and London: Yale University Press, 1988) p. 125.
74. Ibid., p. 128.
75. Judith M. Hughes, *Reshaping the Psychoanalytic Domain: The Work of Melanie Klein, W.R.D. Fairburn, and D.W. Winnicott* (Berkeley, CA: University of California Press, 1989) p. 8.
76. King, p. 129.
77. Melanie Klein, *Love, Guilt and Reparation and Other Works, 1921–1945* (New York: Delacourt Press, 1975); *Envy and Gratitude and Other Works, 1946-1963* (New York: Delacourt, 1975).
78. Hughes, p. 21.
79. King, p. 132.
80. Phyllis Grosskurth, *Melanie Klein: Her World and Her Work* (New York: Knopf, 1986) pp. 281–362. Julia Segal points out Grosskurth's originality in revealing the existence of these Controversial Discussions in *Melanie Klein* (London: Sage Publications, 1992) p. 17.
81. Hughes, p. 26.
82. Michael Fordham, 'Some Historical Reflections,' *Journal of Analytical Psychology*, Vol. 34, No. 3, July 1989, p. 223.
83. Ibid, p. 224.
84. Michael Fordham, 'Analytical Psychology in England,' *Journal of Analytical Psychology*, Vol. 24, No. 4, October 1979, p. 282.
85. Ibid., p. 283.
86. Ibid., pp. 285–7.
87. C.G. Jung, *Civilization in Transition* (Princeton: Princeton University Press, 1964; 2nd edn. 1970) p. 34.
88. Michael Fordham, *Children as Individuals* (New York: G.P. Putnam, 1969) pp. 96–110.
89. James Astor, 'The Emergence of Fordham's Model of Development: A New Integration in Analytical Psychology,' *Journal of Analytical Psychology* Vol. 35, No. 3, July 1990, p. 265.
90. Dorothy Davidson, 'The Child Analytic Training. 1960–1985: The First Quarter Century,' *Journal of Analytical Psychology* Vol. 31, No. 3, July 1986, p. 219.

91. Fordham, 'Some Historical Reflections,' p. 296.
92. Samuels, p. 10.
93. Samuels classifies Lacan as an 'unknowing Jungian' for this reason, p. 10.
94. C.G. Jung, *Symbols of Transformation* (Princeton: Princeton University Press, 1956; 2nd edn 1967) p. 420.
95. Jung, *Archetypes*, p. 96.
96. So see, in *Archetypes*, 'Psychological Aspects of the Mother Archetype,' 'Concerning Rebirth,' 'The Psychology of the Child Archetype,' 'The Psychological Aspects of Kore,' 'The Phenomenology of the Spirit in Fairytales,' 'On the Psychology of the Trickster-Figure,' 'A Study in the Process of Individuation,' and 'Concerning Mandala Symbolism'; and in *Aion*, 'The Shadow,' 'The Syzygy: Anima and Animus,' and 'Christ: A Symbol of the Self.'
97. Jung, *Memories*, p. 391.
98. So see Jung's analysis of dream symbolism in 'The Synthetic or Constructive Method' and 'The Personal and the Collective (or Transpersonal) Unconscious' in *Two Essays*; 'The Phenomenology of the Spirit in Fairytales,' Section II, in *Archetypes*; 'The Nature of Dreams,' 'General Aspects of Dream Psychology,' and 'The Transcendent Function' in *Structure*; and 'The Practical Use of Dream-Analysis' in *The Practice of Psychotherapy*.
99. Samuels, p. 32.
100. Jung, *Aion*, p. 22.
101. Ibid., pp. 37–71.
102. This is countertransference. See Jung, *Practice of Psychotherapy*, pp. 329–38; Fordham, *Jungian Psychotherapy*, pp. 89–96; and Samuels, pp. 187–91.
103. So see, in *Structure*, 'A Review of Complex Theory,' and a long analysis of one complex in 'Psychological Aspects of the Mother Archetype' in *Archetypes*. 'A Study in the Process of Individuation' and 'Concerning Mandala Symbolism' in *Archetypes* are also relevant here, for the first analyzes the appearance of archetypes to a resistant patient and the second includes a discussion of 'disturbed' (or failed) mandalas. See also 'Negative Attempts to Free the Individuality from the Collective Psyche' and 'The Mana-Personality' in *Two Essays*.
104. Jung, *Two Essays*, p. 178.
105. Ibid., p. 179.

106. Ibid., p. 78.
107. William Willeford, *Feeling, Imagination, and the Self: Transformations of the Mother-Infant Relationship* (Evanston, IL: Northwestern University Press, 1988) p. 129.

5 JUNG FOR FEMINISTS

1. Mary Douglas, *Purity and Danger: An Analysis of Concepts of Pollution and Taboo* (New York: Praeger Press, 1966) p. 97, pp. 112–3.
2. C.G. Jung, *Aion: Researches into the Phenomenology of the Self* (Princeton: Princeton University Press, 1959, 2nd edn. 1968) p. 14.
3. C.G. Jung, *Two Essays on Analytical Psychology* (Princeton: Princeton University Press, 1953; 2nd edn. 1966) p. 209.
4. Sydney Janet Kaplan, 'Varieties of Feminist Criticism,' in *Making A Difference: Feminist Literary Criticism*, Gayle Green and Coppélia Kahn (ed.) (London: Methuen, 1985) p. 46; and Judith Kegan Gardiner, 'Mind Mother: Psychoanalysis and Feminism,' in *Making a Difference*, pp. 123–4.
5. Naomi Goldenberg, 'A Feminist Critique of Jung,' *Signs* (1976) 2:2, p. 445; and Estella Lauter and Carol Schreier Rupprecht, (eds), *Feminist Archetypal Theory* (Knoxville: University of Tennessee, 1985) p. 6.
6. Goldenberg, p. 447.
7. Lauter and Rupprecht, p. 10; by implication, Barbara Charlesworth Gelpi, 'The Politics of Androgyny,' *Women's Studies* 2, no. 2 (1974), pp. 151–60.
8. See in C.G. Jung, *Two Essays* (Princeton: Princeton University Press, 1953, 2nd edn. 1966), 'Identification with the Collective Psyche,' 'Phenomena Resulting from the Assimilation of the Unconscious,' 'Attempts to Free the Individuality from the Collective Psyche,' and 'Fundamental Principles in the Treatment of Collective Identity.'
9. Gelpi, p. 158; Annis V. Pratt, *Archetypal Patterns in Women's Fiction* (Bloomington: Indiana University Press, 1981) pp. 7–8, and 'The New Feminist Criticisms: Exploring the History of the New Space,' in *Beyond Intellectual Sexism: A New Reality*, Joan I. Roberts (ed.) New York: McKay Press, 1976) p. 179.

10. C.G. Jung, *Two Essays*, pp. 188–97; *The Archetypes and the Collective Unconscious* (Princeton: Princeton University Press, 1959, 2nd edn. 1968) pp. 26–30; and *Aion*, p. 13.
11. Gelpi, p. 158; and Pratt, *Archetypal Patterns*, p. 7. Although Pratt's estimation of Jung is inadequate, her Jungian book studying the feminine quest for individuation in women's fiction is solid and fine.
12. Goldenberg, p. 449; and Lauter and Rupprecht, throughout.
13. Gelpi, p. 158.
14. Lauter and Rupprecht, pp. 10–13, 226–30.
15. Ibid., p. 226.
16. James Hillman, 'Anima, I,' *Spring* 1973, p. 100.
17. Ibid., p. 109.
18. Ibid., p. 117.
19. C.G. Jung, *Psychology and Religion: West and East* (Princeton: Princeton University Press, 1958, 2nd edn, 1969) pp. 164–92.
20. Nancy Chodorow, 'Gender, Relation, and Difference in Psychoanalytic Perspective,' in *The Future of Difference*, Hester Eisenstein and Alice Jardine (eds) (Boston: G.K. Hall for Barnard Women's Center, 1980) p. 4.
21. Thus Demaris S. Wehr, in *Jung and Feminism: Liberating Archetypes* (Boston: Beacon Press, 1987), considers Jung's psychology to be implicitly sexist because it is concerned with universal archetypes rather than the historical particulars that for women have always included sexism; and her intent is to 'build a bridge between Jung and feminism' (p. x), thus assuming that one must be needed. Compare this with Shelburne's point that social cultures very often affect the forms that archetypes take for individuals, in *Mythos and Logos in the Thought of Carl Jung: The Theory of the Collective Unconscious in Scientific Perspective* (Albany, NY: State University of New York Press, 1988) p. 33.
22. See Domna C. Stanton, 'Language and Revolution: The Franco-American Dis-Connection,' in *The Future of Difference*; Toril Moi, *Sexual/Textual Politics: Feminist Literary Theory* (London and New York: Methuen, 1985) pp. 123–6; and Ann Rosalind Jones, 'Writing the Body: Toward an Understanding of *L'Ecriture Feminin*,' *Feminist Studies* 7 (1981) p. 253.
23. C.G. Jung, *Psychological Types* (Princeton: Princeton University Press, 1921, pub. 1971) p. 400.

24. Jung, *Two Essays*, p. 69.
25. C.G. Jung, *The Structure and Dynamics of the Psyche* (Princeton: Princeton University Press, 1960, 2nd. edn. 1969) p. 156.
26. C.G. Jung, *The Archetypes and the Collective Unconscious* (Princeton: Princeton University Press, 1959, 2nd edn. 1968) p. 79.
27. C.G. Jung, *Civilization in Transition* (Princeton: Princeton University Press, 1964, 2nd edn. 1970) p. 449.
28. Andrew Samuels, *Jung and the Post-Jungians* (London, Boston, Melbourne and Henley: Routledge & Kegan Paul, 1985) p. 25.
29. Shelburne, p. 33.
30. Ibid., p. 55.
31. Chodorow, 'Gender,' p. 4.
32. Ibid.
33. Nancy Chodorow, 'What Is the Relation between Psychoanalytic Feminism and the Psychoanalytic Psychology of Women?' in *Theoretical Perspectives on Sexual Difference*, Deborah L. Rhode (ed.) (New Haven and London: Yale University Press, 1990) p. 118.
34. Nancy Chodorow, *The Reproduction of Mothering: Psychoanalysis and the Sociology of Gender* (Berkeley: University of California Press, 1978) p. 4.
35. Ibid., p. 6.
36. Ibid., pp. 7–9.
37. Chodorow, *Mothering*, p. 167.
38. Ibid., p. 169.
39. Ibid., p. 213.
40. Ibid., p. 215. Chodorow is not alone in suggesting this Utopian solution. See Christiane Olivier, *Jocasta's Children: The Imprint of the Mother*, tr. George Craig (London and New York: Routledge, 1989), who is more vividly direct than Chodorow, and more insightful into adult implications of this pre-Oedipal situation too.
41. Chodorow, *Mothering*, p. 214.
42. Carol Gilligan, *In a Different Voice: Psychological Theory and Women's Development* (Cambridge: Harvard University Press, 1982).
43. Ibid., p. 17.
44. Mary Field Belenky, Blythe McVicker Clinchy, Nancy Rule Goldberger, and Jill Mattuck Tarule, *Women's Ways of Knowing: The Development of Self, Voice, and Mind* (New

York: Basic Books, 1986). This book is the 1987 winner of the Distinguished Publication Award given by the Association of Women in Psychology (United States).

45. Ibid., p. 54.
46. Ibid., p. 55.
47. Ibid., pp. 84–5.
48. C.G. Jung, *Aion*, p. 14.
49. Chodorow, *Mothering*, p. 169.
50. Gilligan, pp. 16–7.
51. Belenky *et al.*, pp.102–3.
52. Michael Fordham is the most prominent member of the Development school: *Children as Individuals* (New York: Putnam, 1969; first published as *The Life of Children*, 1944, by Kegan, Paul, Trench, Trubner & Co.); with R. Gordon, J. Hubback and K. Lambert (eds), *Technique in Jungian Analysis* (London: Heinemann, 1974); and *Jungian Psychotherapy: A Study in Analytical Psychology* (New York: John Wiley & Sons, 1978). Much of the Developmental material has been published in journals, often in *Journal of Analytical Psychology*.
53. Samuels, p. 20.
54. William Willeford, *Feeling, Imagination, and the Self: Transformations of the Mother-Infant Relationship* (Evanston, IL: Northwestern University Press, 1988).
55. Consider the wide range of these articles, published in the *Journal of Analytical Psychology* during the last decade, that relate in some way to women. E.W. Vogelsong, 'The Confrontation Between Lilith and Adam: The Fifth Round,' 30 (April 1985) pp. 149–64; Robert D. Newman, 'The Transformative Quality of the Feminine in the Penelope Episode of *Ulysses*,' 31 (January 1986) pp. 63–74; James Astor, 'Some Aspects of Female Sexuality, Psychopathology, and Their Relation to Infantile States of Mind,' 32 (October 1987) pp. 348–58; M. Vera Bührmann, 'The Feminine in Witchcraft: Part I,' 32 (April 1987) pp. 139–56; 'The Feminine in Witchcraft: Part II,' 32 (July 1987), pp. 257–78; James Astor, 'The Breast as Part of the Whole: Theoretical Considerations Concerning Whole and Part-Objects,' 34 (April 1989) pp. 117–28; Coline Covington, 'In Search of the Heroine,' 34 (July 1989) pp. 243-54; and Varenka Marc, 'Beyond the Archaic Maternal Background,' 36 (April 1991) pp. 231–40.
56. Marcia Westkott, *The Feminist Legacy of Karen Horney* (New

Haven and London: Yale University Press, 1986); Phyllis Grosskurth, *Melanie Klein: Her World and Her Work* (New York: Knopf, 1986); and Janet Sayers, *Mothers of Psychoanalysis: Helene Deutsche, Karen Horney, Anna Freud, and Melanie Klein* (New York: Norton, 1991).

57. Toril Moi, 'Patriarchal Thought and the Drive for Knowledge' in *Between Feminism and Psychoanalysis*, Teresa Brennan (ed.) (New York and London: Routledge & Kegan Paul, 1989) p. 189.
58. Chodorow, 'Gender,' p. 4.
59. Ibid., p. 13.
60. Amy Gross, 'Thinking Like a Woman,' *Vogue*, May 1982, p. 268.
61. Jessica Benjamin, 'Review of *In a Different Voice*,' *Signs* Vol. 9 (Winter 1983), p. 297.
62. Ibid, p. 298.
63. Linda K. Kerber, Catherine G. Greeno and Eleanor E. Maccoby, Zella Luria, Carol B. Stack, and Carol Gilligan, 'On In a Different Voice: An Interdisciplinary Forum,' *Signs*, Vol. 11 (winter 1986), pp. 304–33.
64. Green and Maccoby, p. 308.
65. Kerber, p. 306; and Luria, p. 315.
66. Ibid., p. 318.
67. Gilligan, *Signs* Forum, p. 325.
68. Kerber, p. 306.
69. Green and Maccoby, p. 308; Luria, p. 318.
70. Green and Macoby, p. 315.
71. Jung, *Archetypes*, p. 98.
72. Chodorow, *Mothering*, p. 169.
73. Emma Jung, *Animus and Anima* (Irving, TX: Spring Publications, 1957; 1981). The chapters were originally published as essays ('On the Nature of the Animus,' 1934, and 'The Anima as an Elemental Being,' 1955).
74. Ibid., pp. 4–5, 12–16, and 20–4.
75. M. Esther Harding, *The Way of All Women: A Psychological Interpretation* (New York: G.P. Putnam & Sons, 1970; orig. pub. 1933).
76. Ann Belford Ulanov, *The Feminine in Jungian Psychology and in Christian Theology* (Evanston, IL: Northwestern University Press, 1971) p. 141.
77. Ibid., p. 142.
78. Ibid., p. 146.
79. Jung, *Archetypes*, p. 82.

80. Ulanov, p. 173.
81. Ibid., p. 174.
82. Sherry Turkle, *Psychoanalytic Politics: Freud's French Revolution* (New York: Basic Books, 1978) p. 5.
83. Ibid., p. 6.
84. Ibid., p. 3.
85. Ibid, p. 4.
86. Ibid., p. 11.
87. Ibid., p. 11.
88. Ibid., pp. 196–200.
89. See Luce Irigiray, *This Sex Which Is Not One*, tr. Catherine Porter with Carolyn Burke (Ithaca: Cornell University Press, 1985), pp. 83–102. For the wittiest and most insightful analysis of Irigiray's debunking effort, see Jane Gallop, *The Daughter's Seduction: Feminism and Psychoanalysis* (Ithaca: Cornell University Press, 1982) pp. 80–91.
90. Lacan wrote: 'The phallus is the privileged signifier,' in 'The Signification of the Phallus,' in *Ecrits: A Selection*, tr. Alan Sheridan (New York: Norton, 1977), p. 287.
91. 'Lack' is a packed word that is a favorite in feminist criticism, for it alludes to Freud's and then Lacan's view that women are 'different' because they lack a penis.
92. Hélène Cixous and Catherine Clémente, *The Newly Born Woman*, tr. Betsey Wing (Minneapolis: University of Minnesota Press, 1986; orig. pub. 1975), p. 68.
93. Christiane Makward, 'To Be or Not To Be . . . A Feminist Speaker,' in *Making A Difference*, p. 96.
94. Jane Flax, 'Postmodernism and Gender Relations in Feminist Theory' *Signs* Summer 1987, Vol. 12, no. 4, p. 632; and Jones, 'Writing the Body,' p. 253. Although she does not share this critical assessment, she notes that many feminists hold it.
95. Patricia Yaeger, *Honey-Mad Women: Emancipatory Strategies in Women's Writing* (New York: Columbia University Press, 1988) p. 25.
96. Ann Rosalind, 'Inscribing Femininity: French Theories of the Feminine,' in *Making a Difference*, p. 253.
97. Moi, p. 110.
98. Domna C. Stanton, 'Difference on Trial: A Critique of the Maternal Metaphor in Cixous, Irigiray, and Kristeva,' in *The Poetics of Gender*, Nancy K. Miller (ed.) (New York: Columbia University Press, 1986) p. 161.

99. Betsy Draine, 'Refusing the Wisdom of Solomon: Some Recent Feminist Literary Theory' *Signs*, vol. 15 (Autumn 1989) p. 145.
100. Ibid., p. 146.
101. Ibid., p. 147.
102. Jane Gallop, *Around 1981: Academic Feminist Literary Theory* (New York and London: Routledge, 1992), pp. 41–7.
103. Ibid, p.41; Hélène Cixous, 'The Laugh of the Medusa,' tr. Keith Cohen and Paula Cohen *Signs*, 1976, Vol. 1, no. 4, pp. 875–93.
104. For a good discussion of her non-theoretical writing, see Morag Shiach, *Hélène Cixous: A Politics of Writing* (New York and London: Routledge) 1991. As of this writing, Cixous' latest creative work is her drama, *The Terrible But Unfinished Story of Norodow Sihanouk, King of Cambodia*, tr. Juliet Flower (Lincoln, NE: University of Nebraska Press, 1994).
105. Gallop, *Around 1981*, p. 47.
106. Stanton, 'Language,' pp. 78–9.
107. Yaeger, p. 15.
108. Cixous, p. 885.
109. Elizabeth A. Meese, *Crossing the Double-Cross: The Practice of Feminist Criticism* (Chapel Hill and London: University of North Carolina Press, 1986). See especially Chapter 5, 'Crossing the Double-Cross: the Concept of "Difference" and Feminist Literary Criticism.'
110. Jane Gallop, 'Reading the Mother Tongue: Psychoanalytic Feminist Criticism' *Critical Inquiry* 1987, Vol. 13, no. 2, pp. 314–29. See also Naomi Schor, *Breaking the Chain: Women, Theory, and French Realist Fiction* (New York: Columbia University Press, 1985). She proposes a 'clitoral school of feminist criticism, [that] might then well be identified by its practice of a hermeneutics focused on the detail, which is to say on those details of the female anatomy generally ignored by the male critics' (pp. 159–60).
111. Meese, p. 76.
112. Yaeger, p. 15.
113. Cixous, 'Medusa,' p. 885.
114. But see Susan Rubin Suleiman, 'Writing and Motherhood,' in *The (M)other Tongue*, pp. 252–77.
115. See Jean Hall, *A Mind That Feeds Upon Infinity: The Deep Self in English Romantic Poetry* (Rutherford, Madison, Teaneck: Fairleigh Dickinson University Press, 1991).

116. Julia Kristeva, *Desire in Language: A Semiotic Approach to Language and Literature*, Leon S. Roudiez (ed.) tr. Thomas Gora, Alice Jardin, and Leon S. Roudiez (New York: Columbia University Press, 1980).
117. Gallop, 'Reading the Mother Tongue,' pp. 320–22.
118. Meredith Skura, *The Literary Use of the Psychoanalytic Process* (New Haven: Yale University Press, 1981) p. 85.
119. I suggest a Jungian reading of Shelley's poetry using these theorists in *Shelley's Ambivalence* (London: Macmillan Press, 1989).

6 JUNG FOR THE FUTURE

1. Albert Memmi, *The Colonizer and the Colonized*, tr. Howard Greenfield (New York: Orion Press, 1965; orig. pub. 1957) p. 132.
2. Ibid., pp. ix–xi.
3. Ibid., p. 127ff.
4. Edward W. Said, 'The Politics of Knowledge,' *Raritan*, Vol. XI, 1 (Summer 1991) p. 128.
5. Abdul R. JanMohamed and David Lloyd, 'Preface,' in *The Nature and Context of Minority Discourse*, Abdul R. JanMohamed and David Lloyd (eds.) (New York and Oxford: Oxford University Press, 1991) p. ix.
6. Abdul R. JanMohamed, 'Negating the Negation as a Form of Affirmation in Minority Discourse: The Construction of Richard Wright as Subject,' in *Minority Discourse*, p. 10.
7. Nancy Hartsock, 'Rethinking Modernism: Minority vs. Majority Theories,' in *Minority Discourse*, p. 34.
8. C.G. Jung, *Memories, Dreams, Reflections*, Aniela Jaffé (ed.) (New York: Pantheon Books, 1963), pp. 271–2.
9. Jung, *Memories*, p. 272.
10. C.G. Jung, *The Structure and Dynamics of the Psyche* (Princeton: Princeton University Press, 1960, 2nd edn. 1969) p. 270.
11. Ibid., pp. 61–3.
12. C.G. Jung, *Civilization in Transition* (Princeton: Princeton University Press, 1964; 2nd edn 1970), p. 527.
13. Jung, *Structure*, pp. 261–3.
14. Jung, *Civilization*, pp. 515–34.

15. Edward W. Said, *Orientalism* (New York: Pantheon Books, 1978).
16. Jung, *Civilization*, p. 528.
17. Ibid., pp. 520–2.
18. Ibid., pp. 516–17.
19. Frantz Fanon, *Black Skin, White Masks*, tr. Charles Lam Markmann (New York: Grove Weidenfeld, 1967; orig. pub. 1952).
20. Ibid., p. 522.
21. Ibid., p. 524.
22. Ibid., p. 529.
23. Ibid., p. 518.
24. Jung, *Structure*, p. 226.
25. C.G. Jung, *Two Essays on Analytical Psychology* (Princeton: Princeton University Press, 1953, 2nd edn 1966) p. 178.
26. Bettina L. Knapp, *A Jungian Approach to Literature* (Carbondale and Edwardsville, IL: Southern Illinois University Press, 1984).
27. Ibid., p. x.
28. I include my own book (*Blake and the Assimilation of Chaos*, Princeton: Princeton University Press, 1978) as another illustration of this familiar 'Jungian approach,' written during 1975–7 when myth criticism was in full swing. Its subject is the function that myth-making had for William Blake, which I then saw as his way of incorporating his growing knowledge of the collective unconscious ('chaos') into consciousness.

    Now I would consider different aspects of his situation. Blake certainly was a marginalized figure during his lifetime. He came from a family of hosiers, married an illiterate grocer's daughter, and remained generally poor for all of his life. He was nearly unknown as either artist or poet to his contemporaries. It was not until his early sixties that he began to be appreciated as a great artist by a younger generation of painters led by John Linnell.

    I wonder now how this almost complete marginalization might have affected his poetry and the archetypes manifest in it. What of his fascination with socially marginalized figures that persisted throughout his poetry, and his continuing emphasis that their 'manacles' were really 'mind-forg'd,' as he held in *London*? And what of that arch-enemy in his mythology, Urizen? I noted originally (p. 128) that Urizen faded as a character in the major prophecies as

Blake came to see that the systematizing Urizen is really a mirror-parody of the myth-making Blake: Blake was 'incorporating his Shadow,' as Jung would say. But now I note also that Urizen is portrayed in poem and picture as the Demon-Bogey of patriarchal logocentricism, supreme representative of the dominant imperialist ideology. I wonder now why *he* should be the Double of the marginalized Blake.

29. Jos Van Meurs with John Kidd, *Jungian Literary Criticism 1920–80: An Annotated, Critical Bibliography of Works in English (With a Selection of Titles After 1980)* (Metuchen, N.J., and London: Scarecrow Press, 1988). These four entries are: Stephanie Demetrakopoulos, 'The Metaphysics of Matrilinearity in Women's Autobiography: Studies of Mead's *Blackberry Winter,* Hellman's *Penitents,* Angelou's *I Know Why The Caged Bird Sings,* and Kingston's *The Woman Warrior,*' in *Women's Autobiography: Essays in Criticism,* E. Jelinek (ed.) (Bloomington, IN: Indiana University Press, 1980); William J. Schafer, 'Ralph Ellison and the Birth of the Anti-Hero,' *Studies in Modern Fiction,* Vol. 10, No. 2 (1967–8) pp. 81–93; Marjorie W. McClure, Tucker Orbison, and Philip M. Withim (eds), *The Binding of Proteus: Perspectives on Myth and Literary Process* (Lewisburg, PA: Bucknell University Press, 1980), noted by Van Meurs as containing Jungian-oriented essays on works and authors from medieval romances to LeRoi Jones; Karla Holloway and Stephanie Demetrakopoulos, *New Dimensions of Spirituality: A Biracial and Bicultural Reading of the Novels of Toni Morrison* (Westport, CN: Greenwood Press, 1987).
30. Walter A. Shelburne, *Mythos and Logos in the Thought of Carl Jung: The Theory of the Collective Unconscious in Scientific Perspective* (Albany, NY: State University of New York, 1988) p. 33. 'Different groups assimilate the archetypes into distinct cultural forms, and the phenomenological form of the archetypal images are then a direct result of cultural influence. Moreover, one archetype may be emphasized in one culture but not in another.'
31. Evelyn J. Hinz and John H. Teunissen, 'Culture and the Humanities: The Archetypal Approach,' in *Jungian Literary Criticism,* Richard P. Sugg (ed.) (Evanston, IL: Northwestern University Press, 1992) p. 195.
32. Ibid., p. 197.

33. Jung, *Two Essays*, pp. 139–55, 286–7.
34. One of the best is *Archetypal Patterns in Women's Fiction*, by Annis Pratt with Barbara White, Andrea Loewenstein, and Mary Tyer (Bloomington: Indiana University Press, 1981).
35. Hartsock, p. 34.
36. Shirley Nelson Garner, Claire Kahane, and Madelon Sprengnether (eds), *The (M)other Tongue: Essays in Feminist Psychoanalytic Interpretation* (Ithaca and London: Cornell University Press, 1985) p. 19.
37. Ibid., p. 29.
38. Martha Noel Evans, *Masks of Tradition: Women and the Politics of Writing in Twentieth-Century France* (Ithaca and London: Cornell University Press, 1987) pp. 223–4.
39. Stanton, 'Difference,' p. 174.
40. C.G. Jung, *The Archetypes and the Collective Unconscious* (Princeton: Princeton University Press, 1959; 2nd edn 1968) p. 82.
41. Cixous, 'Medusa,' p. 881.
42. Stanton, 'Difference,' pp. 158–9.
43. Barbara Christian, 'The Race For Theory,' in *Minority Discourse*, pp. 45–6.
44. Memmi, pp. 97–100.
45. Ibid., p. 99.
46. Jung, *Archetypes*, p. 216.
47. Richard Majors and Janet Mancini Billson, *Cool Pose: The Dilemmas of Black Manhood in America* (New York and Ontario: Lexington Books, 1992).
48. Ibid., pp. 57.
49. Ibid., pp. 58–9.

Index